BIBLICAL NATIONHOOD

The Christian imperative of controlled borders

Pastor Peter Simpson
(Minister of Penn Free Methodist Church
in Buckinghamshire)

www.realchristianity.org
www.facebook.com/britainsonlyhope
www.soundcloud.com/penn-free-methodists

BIBLICAL NATIONHOOD
The Christian imperative of controlled borders

Scripture quotations throughout the main text are from
the Authorised (King James) Version of the Bible,
the rights of which are vested in the Crown
and administered by the Crown's patentee,
Cambridge University Press.
Scripture quotations in the foreword are from the English
Standard Version, published by Collins, part of HarperCollins
Publishers.

© Copyright 2024. Pastor Peter Simpson

Proceeds after cost to
Penn Free Methodist Church,
U.K. Registered Charity no. 1138169

Published by PFMC Publications

CONTENTS

Foreword p5

1) The crisis in the U.K. of uncontrolled immigration p8

2) What the Bible teaches about nationhood p20

3) The churches' submission to the globalist agenda of cultural Marxism p45

4) Double Standards p72

5) Failure to integrate p82

6) Summary and Conclusion p98

7) Footnotes/References p103

*The most High
divided to the nations
their inheritance ...
He set the bounds
of the people*

(Deuteronomy 32:8)

BIBLICAL NATIONHOOD : FOREWORD

Some Christians might be surprised to learn that in the final eschatological state of affairs, there still seem to be nations, and even walled cities! As to nations, we find this in places like Revelation 21:23-24 :

"And the city has no need of sun or moon to shine on it, for the glory of God gives it light, and its lamp is the Lamb. By its light will the nations walk ..."

And concerning walled and guarded cities, consider Revelation 22:14-15:

"Blessed are those who wash their robes, so that they may have the right to the tree of life and that they may enter the city by the gates. Outside are the dogs and sorcerers and the sexually immoral and murderers and idolaters, and everyone who loves and practices falsehood."

Yes, Revelation with its rich symbolism can be difficult to fully get our heads around, but it still seems that even with the new heavens and new earth, some semblance of borders and the like will remain. Indeed, the entrance to heaven itself - at least spiritually speaking - is only gained by means of a narrow gate.

It might be objected that things like nations and borders and walls are simply the result of the Fall, and Christians should have nothing to do with them. Regardless of how we understand the world to come, in this current fallen world there certainly is a place for them. There were strict requirements as to who could become a part of God's covenant community in ancient Israel for example.

And simply having a need for civil government in this sin-soaked world presupposes things such as boundaries, protections, restrictions, and prohibitions of various sorts. For example, at least two of the Ten Commandments (on theft and coveting) presuppose private property, and things like walls or fences or barriers are part of how such property is kept safe.

The Biblical and theological case for all this, along with the social and political case, is very nicely made in this helpful book. Pastor Simpson aptly brings together Christian and non-Christian material and arguments to make a solid case for why we must resist the siren calls of the secular and religious left on these matters.

He makes it clear that of course we are to show proper love and respect for our neighbours, whether in our own local area or among the nations. But that does NOT mean that we simply run with open slather in terms of who wants to enter a nation, any more than we foolishly demand that all homeowners throw open their doors and windows, allowing anyone in for any reason.

Indeed, the wealthier some of these leftists are, the more likely they will have very elaborate and very expensive security systems set up, complete with cameras, direct links to security companies, and plenty of high walls and guarded fences. Are they all being immoral, unloving, and un-Christlike, by having these locks and other security measures?

Protecting one's nation is an outgrowth of protecting one's family and one's community. A genuine and Biblical love of neighbour can and should coexist with these realities. Indeed, it is a LACK of neighbourly love that allows porous or open borders, which put our neighbours and citizens at genuine risk. It is not just a loss of jobs, but a loss of life that too often is the outcome of these flawed policies.

The Christian case for all this needs to be made, and that is just what we find here in this well-researched, well-written and Biblically-based book. Well done Pastor Simpson.

Bill Muehlenberg, Australian-based author, lecturer and blogger at CultureWatch: **https://billmuehlenberg.com/**

Chapter One

THE CRISIS IN THE U.K. OF UNCONTROLLED IMMIGRATION

It is the plain teaching of the Bible that all people are equal in the sight of God, and that the kingdom of God, the community of true believers in Christ, is made up of people of every tribe and tongue from all over the world. Furthermore, both as an obligation and as a delight the Christian loves his neighbour, whoever he is and wherever he comes from. These are primary truths, which this writer resolutely upholds.

Many churches, however, have abused these truths, using them to justify the abandonment of the very concept of nationhood. They have embraced instead the New Age and Marxist idea that a 'global village' world order with no national border controls is a worthy objective which must be pursued as a moral imperative.

In adopting these ideas, the churches have conformed to secular, not Biblical thinking. By constantly supporting the very principle of mass immigration and cultural and ethnic diversity, they have simply mimicked the all-prevailing cultural Marxism of our time. Conformity to man-made philosophy, however, is explicitly condemned in God's word, in Romans 12:2, 1 Corinthians 3:19 and

Colossians 2:8.

In the year 2022 net migration into the U.K. reached the level of 745,000 people [1]. This figure represents a 20% increase from the year to June 2022. Over the past 20 years the U.K. population has risen by nearly 7 million people, or 7 times the population of Birmingham [2]. In the year to June 2023, net migration reached 672,000. The Migration Watch think tank states concerning these figures, "If the current state of influx continues, Britain's population could sky-rocket to 85 million by 2046, a rise equivalent to 18 new cities the size of Birmingham" [3].

The pressures which this creates on hospitals, doctors' surgeries, the schools, the nation's housing stock and general infrastructure are enormous. It is estimated that the U.K. will need "8,010 new schools, 3,168 more GP surgeries, 162 hospitals, 90 universities, 90 Police stations and 19 colleges" by 2046 to accommodate these levels of growth [4]. Even before the net migration figure of 672,000 for the year to June 2023 was known, it was reckoned that a new home needs to be built "every five minutes, day and night, just for new arrivals (into the country)" [5]. Where are all these new homes supposed to be put in this already overcrowded island of ever-dwindling countryside?

Every year in Britain the headlines speak of a looming crisis within the NHS because of so much pressure upon the hospitals' limited resources [6]. Patients who need emergency treatment frequently have to wait over 12 hours to be dealt with [7]. Yet despite these stark realities, those who speak out demanding that migration levels be severely restricted are still deemed to be far-right extremists.

Gross inward migration in the year 2022 amounted to 1.2 million people [8]. In the same year 30.3% of all births in England and Wales were to foreign-born women [9]. This is up from 28.2% in 2016 [10]. In 2021 the census revealed that white Britons made up only 37% of the nation's capital city, 43% of Birmingham, and 49% of Manchester [11]. These figures represent a sizeable fall from the figures available in 2016. In other words, the changing nature and identity of the country is now taking place at a fast rate. This means that these figures on the proportion of indigenous citizens living in England's major cities have probably decreased even more as this book is being written. Are these developments the ultimate God-pleasing virtue which our society is under a moral obligation to pursue?

It also needs to be asked, Is there any African, Asian, Middle Easter or South American country which would heartily welcome such trends, and which is doing all that it can to bring about the dilution of its national identity through continuing and overwhelming levels of immigration? The answer of course is, No.

At the time of writing there is also growing concern in Ireland about the large levels of both legal and illegal migration into the country which are becoming obvious for all to see [12]. To those who claim that people in Britain who want immigration severely reduced are revealing their bigotry and prejudice, would they likewise claim that the people of Ireland are not entitled to their own homeland, and should therefore stop their racist complaints about the high levels of migrant entry

10

into their country?

In 2023 on the official website of the Mayor of London there appeared a photograph of a white family. The caption to the photo said of the family that it 'doesn't represent real Londoners'. How insulting is that to indigenous English people living in their own capital city? Furthermore, it was reported in January 2024 that a recent advert for a vacant position with Transport for London stated that applicants would only be considered, if they belonged to an ethnic minority [13]. Again, how utterly insulting and offensive this is to English Londoners. These two incidents provide a good example of the unhealthy environment which mass immigration has helped to bring about.

As just stated, Britain, which is already suffering from severe strains on housing supply, infrastructure and public services, is allowing well in excess of a million people to cross its borders in a single year. Why is this? The answer is because of the spirit of the age which is dominated by the philosophies of anti-Christian, anti-nation, cultural Marxism.

Is there a God-given universal law established for all time, that whilst all the peoples of the earth are entitled to distinctive national and cultural identities, Britain and the nations of Western Europe are of necessity the exceptions to this rule? Of course not.

The immigration issue brings into sharp focus the whole question of what a nation is. In discussing this, we enter into a highly sensitive area in which it is easy to be misunderstood. So the reader's forbearance is requested as an attempt is made to reach a distinctly Biblical perspective. Rushing to call someone 'racist', just because he advocates strict controls of the nation's borders is not an honourable means of carrying on a debate.

The contention of this book is that it is neither immoral nor 'un-Christian' to question the great migrant influx into Britain of recent decades, nor is it remotely unfriendly to individual immigrants, amongst whom this author has as many fine friends and acquaintances as anyone else. Furthermore, it is the case that various people of immigrant backgrounds are themselves astonished and perplexed at Britain's failure to control its borders properly. Are these immigrants to be denounced as racists as well?

Liberal secularism's political correctness in welcoming mass immigration, and in treating the acceptance of it as the essence of all that is good, has helped to create a very unhealthy environment whereby vast numbers of people are actually frightened to disagree with the liberal orthodoxy. Many are even being tempted to abandon rational, common sense thinking, so afraid are they of being called 'racist' by cultural Marxism's thought police, who have something of a stranglehold over the media and most of our national institutions.

This fear is particularly seen in the horrific sexual grooming scandals which have taken place in the U.K. in recent years (going back to the 1980s) in which the victims were mainly white girls and the perpetrators were generally non-white adult males, mostly of Pakistani origin. This crisis of criminality was first exposed in the Yorkshire town of Rotherham in 2012, but the evil had never been properly dealt for many years by the Police and Social Services there, so afraid were they of being branded as racists or Islamophobes [14]. In other words, those in positions of responsibility and able to help the victims of sordid crime were overcome with irrational fear of being called racist, simply because the criminals involved did not have a white skin.

The Jay Report commissioned by Rotherham Borough Council to look into the problems of child sexual exploitation in the town concluded that at least 1400 girls had been victims of abuse between 1997 and 2013. The report stated concerning the professionals who should have been protecting the children that, "several staff described their nervousness about identifying the ethnic origins of perpetrators for fear of being thought as racist; others remembered clear direction from their managers not to do so" [15].

Rochdale and Telford have also been major centres of similar grooming gang activity. Thankfully, in more recent times (Spring 2023) a U.K. Home Secretary faced up to the primary ethnic origin of the criminal gangs, along with the stark reality that their victims were white girls. Surely there should be universal outrage at the distinctly racist character of the activity of these gangs, but in fact the Home Secretary (who no longer holds that office) was accused instead of "amplifying far-right narratives" [16]. So this is where we are in modern Britain : to identify criminality in which the offenders are non-white and their victims are indigenous Britons is deemed to be a disreputable act of far-right bigotry.

Journalist and author, Douglas Murray, wrote in 2017 in his book, 'The Strange Death of Europe : Immigration, Identity, Islam',

"The identity and ideology of Europe have become about 'respect', 'tolerance' and (most self-abnegating of all) 'diversity'. Such shallow self-definitions ... have no chance at all of being able to call on the deeper loyalties that societies must be able to reach, if they are going to survive for long. This is just one reason why it is likely that our European culture, which has lasted all these centuries ... will not survive" [17].

This is a good summary of the problem which we are up against in contemporary Britain because of uncontrolled immigration, along with the philosophical environment created by the politicians, media and educational establishment, backed up by big business, which declares that even to question the eye-watering levels of nation-transforming immigration must of necessity be a shameful and immoral act.

One might add to Douglas Murray's astute observation here that the ultimate cause of this profound malaise of the complete failure by the leaders and opinion formers within British society to understand what nationhood is all about is their abandonment of the unique and precious Christian revelation as set forth in the Bible. God is not mocked, and He gives up those who refuse to acknowledge His authority to a spiritual and philosophical blindness which will lead to their ultimate downfall :

"Even as they did not like to retain God in their

knowledge, God gave them over to a reprobate mind ... without understanding" (Romans 1:28, 31).

"Reprobate mind" in that quotation refers to a mind which has failed the test and which no longer functions as it ought to do. The Bible is the inerrant word of God. It deals with every aspect of human existence. Accordingly, the concepts of nationhood and national borders are themselves an aspect of the Biblical revelation, as we shall set out to demonstrate. Yet the churches have imitated the liberal, secularist establishment, immersed as it is in the anti-Christian creed of cultural Marxism, in arguing that vast influxes of people of different races, cultures, backgrounds and ethnic origins can only always be beneficial, and what is more, it is a moral imperative incumbent upon all Christians to promote and welcome such developments.

We live in an age where there is great concern about 'saving the planet' and 'protecting the environment'. This presumably ought to include a desire in a British context of protecting the nation's ever dwindling rural environment from being concreted over. One of the primary generators of this demand is indisputably ever increasing immigration. As most immigrants (though obviously not all) settle in England (over 90% [18]), there is a particular danger of the English countryside fast disappearing, along with the destruction of its precious agricultural capacity, which is itself a wonderful providential blessing from God.

How fashionable it is to have concern for preserving natural habitats and the environment generally, but how readily these concerns seem to be laid to one side in any

15

conversation about the enormous ongoing levels of immigration. A major reason for this is of course is that most people are too scared to challenge the woke orthodoxy about immigration only ever having positive and beneficial results, along of course with the fear of most over being called racist, if they dare to question the principle of ongoing high levels of entry.

So it needs repeating, in the current situation whereby open debate on these issues is always hindered by charges of bigotry and xenophobia, that to advocate sensible and strict border controls, and the need to preserve the indigenous culture and identity, has absolutely nothing to do with being far-right or racist. However, in modern Britain vast numbers of well educated and otherwise reasonable people have had their minds so fashioned by years of propaganda from the liberal establishment that they think that it must of necessity be racist for a country to introduce very strict immigration controls.

It is a plain fact that England's population density is now higher than India's, the nation with the second highest population in the world, and the density is also 3.5 times more than that of France [19]. England is in fact the most densely populated European country, except for Malta [20]. From June 2011 to June 2015 around 2.2 million National Insurance (NI) numbers were handed out to migrants from the European Union [21]. In the year to January 2017 683,000 NI numbers were issued to adult overseas nationals [22]. In the year to June 2023 the figure rose to 1.1 million, which was a rise from 880,000 in the year to June 2022 [23]. The 1.1 million figure represents the highest number since figures were

16

first published in 2002.

Can anyone reasonably argue that these figures do not effect the ability of those already resident in the U.K. to find work, have a downward effect on wage levels, and cause increasing strains on the U.K. infrastructure? It also appears that Britain's departure from the European Union has done nothing to reduce the enormous ongoing levels of inward migration, despite the fact that the result of the 2016 referendum on EU membership constituted a rejection of the open borders/free movement of peoples philosophy so integral to the EU.

Such levels of immigration are quite unsustainable in basic, practical and physical terms, as well as in respect of the more complex issues of integration/non-integration of the new arrivals. Must we just accept it as 'normal' that our culture and identity, not to mention our distinctly Christian foundations, are going to be irredeemably removed for evermore, because our political 'betters' consider it good for us? What civilisation in human history has adopted, when not forced to, such a hopelessly defeatist attitude to its own identity and existence?

As we have stated, for the last 60 years the churches have consistently taken a pro-immigration stance. A common argument used to justify the current enormous levels of migration has been that Britain has always been a nation of immigrants. Such an argument, however, is completely untenable, because it ignores facts such as the following, laid out in a concise and summary format (and some of the details of which have been stated above) :

- In the decade from 2001 to 2011 the Government allowed the population, through immigration, to grow at a faster rate than at any time since the first ever census conducted in 1801 [24].
- 3.6 million migrants entered the U.K. between 1997 and 2010 [25].
- In London in 2021 nearly two-thirds of the population was not white British, which category then represented only 36.8% of the total [26].
- Net migration in 2022 reached the figure of 745,000 people, whilst gross migration amounted to 1.16 million people [27]
- In the year to June 2023, net migration reached 672,000 [28], whilst gross migration amounted to 1.2 million [29].
- Each new set of annual immigration statistics must not be considered in a vacuum, but as a compounding of what has been going for many years previously.
- "The existing migrant population will in future have even greater housing needs as compared to the rest of the population due to their relatively young age structure" [30].
- In the year to June 2022 approximately 10,388,000 people in England and Wales were not born in the U.K.. This figure equals some 14.8% of the population [31].

No immigration in Britain's long history is anywhere near the levels indicated in the above statistics. It is again to be asserted most strongly that as Christians we love our neighbour, whoever he is and wherever he comes from, but that does not mean that we must ignore the difficulties which large-scale immigration brings, such as wage depression amongst the lower paid, pressures on public services, the destruction of the countryside - because of the need for ever more housing and infrastructure - and the cultural transformation of neighbourhoods and indeed of the very character and identity of the nation itself.

There are now towns and cities in the U.K. where the schoolchildren speak up to 150 different languages [32]. This must be an educational nightmare. What are the supposed benefits of such a situation meant to be? In London an incredible figure of 300 different languages are spoken [33].

No one can argue that large-scale immigration does not lead to major cultural, religious and social change in a nation. Is it sinful even to question the inevitable transformation which is taking place in modern Britain? Are there specific and irrefutable Scripture passages teaching us that cultural diversification by means of mass immigration is God's imperative for the nations? The plain answer is : most definitely not. Yet the churches have given the impression that to 'embrace diversity' through lax border controls is a moral obligation before God.

Therefore the levels of migratory influx which Britain has experienced for many decades now must not automatically be regarded by Christians as somehow possessing great virtue in God's sight. There is nothing remotely wrong with a national government putting the needs of its own citizens first, and in giving priority to the retention of its own cultural identity, any more than it is wrong for a father in managing his income and household to put the needs of his own family first.

19

Chapter Two

WHAT THE BIBLE SAYS ABOUT NATIONHOOD

The divine institution of nationhood goes right back to Genesis chapter 10, where we read of "the generations of the sons of Noah, Shem, Ham and Japheth" who would form the basis of the various different nations in the future history of the world. In a section about the descendants of Noah's son Ham, we read,

"The border of the Canaanites was from Sidon, as thou comest to Gerar, unto Gaza; as thou goest, unto Sodom, and Gomorrah, and Admah, and Zeboim, even unto Lasha. These are the sons of Ham, after their families, after their tongues, in their countries, and in their nations" (Genesis 10:19–20).

The text then speaks of the descendants of Noah's son Shem, of whom we are told,

"Their dwelling was from Mesha, as thou goest unto Sephar a mount of the east. These are the sons of Shem, after their families, after their tongues, in their lands, after their nations"
(Genesis 10:30–31).

So very early on in the Bible we have a reference to the peoples of the world being divided up into separate nations. However, the formation of nations described in Genesis 10 is looking forward in time. There was not an immediate acceptance of the principle of living in distinctive national groups, but there was rather a rebellion against such a prospect, which stemmed from a rebellion against the authority of God generally. We read of the peoples inhabiting the earth in these early post-Flood days in Genesis 11,

"*They said, Go to, let us build us a city and a tower, whose top may reach unto heaven; and let us make us a name, **lest we be scattered abroad upon the face of the whole earth***" *(Genesis 11:4).*

Satanic inspired false religion had taken hold of these people. They turned to the worship of the stars and other created objects. The Tower of Babel was built as a mighty symbol of their human solidarity and of their desire not to be dispersed over the earth into separate national groups, as God required of them. Thus in defiance of their Maker they refused to spread out across the earth. Instead, they desired to create a single empire, seeking their strength and security in their human togetherness. The Lord therefore confounded their languages, so that they had no choice but to disperse into separate units on the basis of their tongues.

So we see from this early phase of human history that the Lord was actually imposing nationhood because of mankind's wayward behaviour. Because all men are fallen and in rebellion against God, nationhood is God's chosen method of ordering His world.

The integrity of national boundaries and the need to

respect them is clearly taught in Scripture. It is implicit in the injunctions of the law of Moses to respect tribal and family boundaries, for example :

"Thou shalt not remove thy neighbour's landmark" (Deuteronomy 19:14).

In Deuteronomy 32:8 Moses tells us that, just as the Lord separated the nation of Israel, so He also ordained the independent existence of all the other nations. He declares,

"When the most High divided to the nations their inheritance, when he separated the sons of Adam, he set the bounds of the people according to the number of the children of Israel" (Deuteronomy 32:8).

So God created all the other nations with a view to His specific purpose for the nation of Israel. Let us in particular note the wording here : **"The most High divided to the nations their inheritance ... He set the bounds of the people"**. Here is God's own stamp upon the legitimacy of nationhood and national borders.

In 1942, in the midst of the Second Word War, there was a book published by the Christian minister and author, Harry Lacey, and it was entitled *God and the Nations*. As with most books, one does not agree with absolutely everything it says, but this writer would like to acknowledge its helpfulness in setting out the Biblical teaching on nationhood. At the time of its publication many countries in Europe had fallen to the Nazis, and others were embroiled in a horrible ongoing conflict. The book asks the questions, Despite this world war, is God still governing the earth and working out His purposes?, and, What is His attitude to the nations and to nationhood itself?

Mr Lacey writes, and this will surprise and even shock many, *"National barriers proceed from God, who ... departmentalises the human race, rather than communising it. The idea of one community of men ... is foreign to the Bible"* [34].

Lest there be any confusion here, we emphasise that we are not discussing the Church, the one universal body of Christ, which of course comprises all peoples, whatever their nationality and ethnic origin, but the arrangement of human societies here on earth. It is of course the case that all men are descended from Adam and all are made of one blood (Acts 17:26). Therefore all share a common humanity and a total equality under God, but those truths in no way undermine the fact that the Lord Himself has ordained the existence of separate nations as an aspect of His purposes for the fallen human race.

With the coming of the Lord Jesus Christ the theocracy which was Israel ceased to exist, and the Son of God established in His death, resurrection and ascension a kingdom which is not of this world. Indeed, the theocracy began to enter into its death throes some 600 years earlier with the fall of Jerusalem in 586BC. This was the start of the preparation for the setting up of the messianic kingdom which is not of this world, the Israel of God made up of the redeemed out of every nation, and with its citizenship in heaven. This is most definitely a community comprising people of every tribe and tongue.

However, nationhood per se in terms of how God orders a fallen world was never abolished under the new covenant. It is in precisely in this area that the thinking in many churches has gone seriously awry. The disciples of Christ are instructed to preach "repentance and remission of sins ... in his name among all nations" (Luke 24:27), not to declare to the world that those nations should no longer exist, or that they are morally inferior institutions. The new covenant introduced the abolition of the Jew-Gentile distinction (Galatians 3:28) in terms of how to identify the people of God, but not the ending of God's own ordinance of nationhood comprising, as it does, a distinct identity and clearly defined and controlled borders.

Mr Lacey writes in the aforementioned book that as we study God's word,

"We shall be surprised how much light is given on the ways of God with the nations, and how clearly He sets forth His principles and purposes. The Scriptures explain the origin of nations and the apportioning of their lands (and) the secrets of the rise and fall of kingdoms and empires" [35].

We find the origin of nations in Genesis chapters 9,10 and 11. The sons of Noah after the Flood were told to go forth and to multiply across the whole earth. In chapter 10 we actually have set down the origin of 58 separate and distinct nations. Around 100 years after the Flood a rebellious generation of men in the plain of Shinar tried to communise themselves into a single unit. This was all a fruit of their worship of false gods, and the one true God had to intervene to frustrate their multi-faith, unifying plans for a single world empire. He therefore confounded their language, so that they were forced to disperse all over the earth into separate language groups inhabiting separate regions.

Remaining in the book of Genesis, we read in chapter 30,

"It came to pass, when Rachel had born Joseph, that Jacob said unto Laban, Send me away, that I may go unto mine own place, and to my country" (Genesis 30:25).

Here we see Jacob desiring to return to the land of his birth. He calls it 'his own place'. He has been living in Mesopotamia for 14 years, but Canaan is still 'his own place'. So we see here a man of God speaking of the reality of his national identity and native affiliation.

Jacob's return to Canaan was of course all part of the unfolding of God's plan of salvation for mankind, a plan which centred upon the very institution of nationhood. Indeed, for 2000 years from the time of Abraham God would specifically use nationhood in the unfolding of His glorious scheme of redemption for the world. This fact alone proves that nationhood cannot be intrinsically wrong or morally defective.

Mr Lacey further states concerning the differing features of geography and climate of the various regions of the world in the post-Flood period, *"It is probable that (the) earth was prepared thus with a view to separating the sons of Adam and moving the different families to as many different lands, that there each in its own inheritance might become a nation with its own individuality and live out its national experience before*

God" [36].

Scripture is the authority for this conclusion, because the Trinitarian God is He who in His omnipotence ordains the circumstances of men. So the development of distinct national identities, characteristics and destinies, often shaped by geography and climate, is all part of the overall providence of God. For example, that Britain is an island is an aspect of God's providence which has played a key role in our history, and indeed survival, as a nation. It is simply not Biblical to argue, as many in the churches do, that the erosion of national identity and sovereignty in favour of a global coming together is somehow a glorious Christian objective.

In Numbers 20 and 21 we read of the Israelites travelling from the wilderness to the Promised Land. They needed to pass through the territory belonging to the Edomites and the Amorites. So they asked the kings of these two nations for permission to travel through their lands. Moses, led by the Holy Spirit, told the kings that his people would not stray from the main highway, nor touch any crops, because they did not belong to Israel. Moses even offered to pay for any water that Israel's cattle consumed in transit. He thus carefully observed the Edomites' and Amorites' boundaries as being ordained of God, and worthy of all respect.

"Let us pass, I pray thee, through thy country; we will not pass through the fields, or through the vineyards, neither will we drink of the water of the wells; we will go by the king's high way, we will not turn to the right hand nor to the left, until we have passed thy borders" (Numbers 20:17).

Notice here how Moses, led by the Holy Spirit, uses the expressions "thy country" and "thy borders", when speaking to the king of Edom. He assures the king that the Israelites will behave with a particular deference, until such time as they "have passed his borders".

Applying this principle to our own day, we learn that to control a nation's borders, and to respect the borders of other nations, is righteous behaviour in the sight of God.

This means that illegal entry into this country, such as is happening virtually every day across the English Channel as this author writes, is sinful and contrary to God's purposes. It demonstrates a lack of respect for the borders which God has ordained.

Concerning the need for the Israelites to respect the Edomites and the integrity of their national borders, the Lord told Moses told in Deuteronomy 2:5,

"Meddle not with them; for I will not give you of their land, no, not so much as a foot breadth; because I have given mount Seir unto Esau for a possession" (Deuteronomy 2:5).

Once again we have a statement here of the principle of God Himself determining which peoples occupy the various regions of the earth's surface, and the need for all the other peoples to respect what He has ordained.

The scholars C.F. Keil and F. Delitzsch were the authors of what have been described as "the great evangelical commentaries of the entire Old Testament ... (Their work) represents the best of evangelical scholarship of the 19th century" [37]. Amongst their comments on the above-quoted text of Deuteronomy 2:5, referring to the people journeying through the wilderness, we read, "The Lord commanded (the Israelites) to turn northwards, i.e. to go round the southern end of Mount Seir and proceed northwards on the eastern side of it without going to war with the Edomites, as He would not give them a foot-breadth of their land, for He had given Esau (i.e. the Edomites) Mount Seir for a possession" [38].

So we observe here how Keil and Delitzsch rightly describe the sovereignty of God in apportioning a specific territory to a specific people. Concerning Deuteronomy 32:8, quoted above (**"The most High divided to the nations their inheritance ... He set the bounds of the people"**), Keil and Delitzsch write that these words, "are not to be restricted to the one confusion of tongues and division of the nations as described in Genesis 11, but embrace the whole period of the development of the one human family in separate tribes and nations, together with their settlement in different lands, for it is no doctrine that the division of the nations was completed once for all" [39]. In other words, the principle of the dividing of the nations was an ongoing one, not merely a single historical event as a result of the Tower of Babel affair.

The two Old Testament scholars further state, "The Scriptures show that, like the formation of the nations from families and tribes, the possession of the lands by the nations so formed was to be traced to God - (it) was the work of divine providence and government" [40].

In Acts 17:26 Paul writes, *"(God) hath made of one blood all nations of men for to dwell on all the face of the earth, and hath determined the times before appointed, and the bounds of their habitation"*.

This text shows us how the Bible combines the fact of our common humanity with the existence of distinct nations, whereas liberal secularism, supported by very many churches, argues that common humanity must of necessity negate nationhood. Let us note here how Paul, inspired by the Holy Spirit, plainly re-asserts in a New Testament context the Old Testament teaching that nationhood and definitive national boundaries are decreed by the Lord.

In Genesis 42 we read of Joseph's brothers travelling down into Egypt because of the famine in Canaan. Little did they realise that their young brother, whom they had sold into slavery 20 years earlier, was now Egypt's first minister. The brothers had treated Joseph with appalling malice back then. Joseph recognises them, but they do not recognise him. He of course has special issues with them because of their previous mis-treatment of him, and so he does not welcome them with open arms. Are they still of the same malicious spirit of all those years previously? He needs to test them. He says to them,

"Ye are spies; to see the nakedness of the land ye are come. And they said unto him, Nay, my lord, but to buy food are thy servants come. We are all one man's sons; we are true men, thy servants are no spies. And (Joseph) said unto them … Hereby ye shall be proved : By the life of Pharaoh ye shall not go forth hence, except your youngest brother come hither. Send one of you, and let him fetch your

brother, and ye shall be kept in prison, that your words may be proved, whether there be any truth in you : or else by the life of Pharaoh surely ye are spies" (Genesis 42:9-16).

There is still one young brother at home, Benjamin, also a son of Rachel, as Joseph was. Joseph needs to know if the brothers are as resentful towards Benjamin, as they once were towards him.

So there are very special circumstances behind Joseph's treatment of his brothers. Nevertheless, he was also a righteous man before God, and the way in which he conducts himself towards his brothers was in accordance with the existing protocols of his high office in Egypt, and to which God had appointed him. He questions closely the identity of the foreigners entering into the land, even when they claim to being doing so only because they are in great need. So what we in fact observe here is Joseph, as Egypt's first minister, strictly controlling the integrity of Egypt's borders, which was a major aspect of the duties of his role in the government of the nation.

A commentator on this passage states, "Such an arrival … (from abroad) as that of Joseph's brethren would be a matter of state, worthy of the attention of the highest officials; and probably (the brothers) had themselves come prepared to be assailed with the accusation of having political objects in view in their visit" [41]. In other words, Joseph was behaving as any nation's leader was expected to do. Since time immemorial governments have seen the essential nature of controlled borders (Joseph was heading up the government of Egypt in around 3,700BC). It has only been in the late 20th and early 21st centuries in the Western world, and in the context of a wholesale departure from Christian foundations, that the principle of carefully controlled borders has been abandoned.

Nor is the principle of unapologetically adhering to a distinctive national identity contrary to Biblical teaching, as contemporary 'woke' philosophy would have us believe. For example, after his conversion to Christ, the apostle Paul never lost his profound sense of identity with his own people. He remained a Jew through and through. He declared,

"I say the truth in Christ, I lie not, my conscience also bearing me witness in the Holy Ghost, that I have great heaviness and continual sorrow in my heart ... for my brethren, my kinsmen according to the flesh" (Romans 9:1-4).

So Paul poured out his heart to God in concern for his own countrymen. How Britain today needs Christians with a similar Spirit-given burden for their nation.

John Wesley wrote, *"We feel in ourselves a strong ... kind of natural affection for our country, which we apprehend Christianity was never designed either to root out or to impair"* [42]. What an amazingly non-pc statement! Christianity was never designed to destroy national identity! John Knox famously prayed, *"Lord, give me Scotland or I die"*. He was being Biblical. He had a profound concern that his own people might be delivered from spiritual darkness, and in this he was emulating, for example, Jeremiah in his special burden for the people of Judah.

As we today look at the godlessness around us, with our society increasingly turning its back upon the one true faith of Christ, and as we look at the indigenous population's appalling descent into unbelief and rebellion against God's word, we desperately need Christians with an unashamedly national perspective, with a burden for their country and for their people's standing before the holy God. (This of course does not exclude a burden for other peoples as well).

There are a number of references in Scripture relating to Israel and 'strangers'. In these it is clearly taught that the strangers must be treated well. For example we read in Jeremiah,

"Do no wrong, do no violence to the stranger, the fatherless, nor the widow, neither shed innocent blood in this place" (Jeremiah 22:3).

The point of injunctions like these is that the strangers are seen as vulnerable individuals, often being listed alongside the fatherless and widows. Indeed, in no less than 18 Old Testament verses the stranger, the fatherless and the widow are referred to in the same breath. Any nation in any age will always find small numbers of strangers/foreign people in its midst, and such should be afforded courtesy, respect and equal treatment under the law.

To argue from these 'stranger' passages, however, that it is immoral so much as to question the arrival of whole communities of incomers, comprising tens and hundreds of thousands, is a conclusion without any contextual warrant.

Furthermore, one cannot claim from Scripture that a broadly ethnocentric basis to nationhood (with respect and equal treatment for all others) is intrinsically sinful. If it were sinful, then the Lord would not have used the ethnocentric nation of Israel to fulfil His purposes of redemption for the world for 2,000 years from the time of Abraham to the time of Christ.

As already intimated, it is also not legitimate to use 'Gentile-inclusive' texts such as Galatians 3:28 to justify the obliteration of national identity. When Paul says, *"In Christ there is neither Jew nor Greek"*, he is stating that men of every nation may be partakers of the covenant of grace, and belong to Christ's spiritual kingdom, not that nationhood upon earth should be abolished.

In Romans 3:29 the apostle Paul asks :

"Is he the God of the Jews only? is he not also of the Gentiles? Yes, of the Gentiles also".

So, says Paul, the God of Israel is not just the God of a single nation, but also of the whole earth encompassing every single other nation. The Greek word translated Gentiles is 'ethnos', from which we derive our word 'ethnicity', and it can with equal accuracy be translated 'nations'. The Lord, who in the Old Testament period gave a special role in His redemptive purposes to one particular nation, has always remained at the same time the God of all nations. Romans 3:29, therefore, is a confirmation, if one were needed, that He continues to be sovereign over all countries and their rulers right now in our own times.

There is absolutely no suggestion by Paul that nations should never have existed in the first place, or that with the coming of Christ they have become defunct, or that they are now ethically dubious when compared to federations in which national distinctions are removed. This has to be emphasised, because the power of secular political correctness has deceived many in the churches into thinking that there is something distinctly 'un-Christian' about nationhood, as opposed to great unions of diverse peoples.

So there is nothing remotely immoral or 'un-Christian' about a nation controlling its borders, or deporting those who are not entitled to be in the country. Yet in modern Britain someone can enter into the country illegally, have their asylum application rejected, and yet still receive short-term housing, help with medical prescriptions, dental care and eyesight, and a payment card for food and toiletries [43]. Surely this is to reward premeditated law-breaking. The Bible makes it clear that the laws of the land must be respected as a Christian duty, and so Christians in particular should not be condoning illegal entry into Britain. This needs to be said, because the teachings of cultural Marxism have swamped Christian thinking in recent years.

Because of the enormous influence of Biblical Christianity there is something very special about the United Kingdom, and about the way in which it has developed over the last 500 years since the time of the Protestant Reformation. What is so special about is the enormous purifying and beneficial influence of the gospel of Jesus Christ. This, above anything else, has fashioned all that is good about our society, identity and culture. This is because it is the Trinitarian God who governs the nations and determines their destinies according to His unchanging law. Even today, the residual effects of our Bible-based civilisation are being benefitted from. This is what makes the country so attractive a destination for people who live in lands where other religions prevail.

This reality of God's moral government of the nations is brought out very clearly in Isaiah chapter 3, of which the Bible commentator Matthew Henry (1662-1714) states, "O that the nations of the earth at this day would hearken to rebukes and warnings which this chapter gives" [44]. Here Henry rightly stresses that God's dealings with Old Testament Israel and other Old Testament nations give us vital guidance for His dealings with the nations today. In Isaiah chapter 3 the prophet declares of his own nation :

"For Jerusalem is ruined, and Judah is fallen: because their tongue and their doings are against the Lord ... they declare their sin as Sodom, they hide it not. Woe unto their soul! for they have rewarded evil unto themselves" (Isaiah 3:8–9).

So we see there that God brings down proud nations which reject His commandments; but the the converse is true as well : He grants earthly blessings to nations which honour Him. This is plainly taught by Solomon in the book of Proverbs:

"Righteousness exalteth a nation, but sin is a reproach to any people" (Proverbs 14:34).

"By the blessing of the upright the city is exalted" (Proverbs 11:11).

The Lord's providential control over national prosperity and social stability is also made clear in Psalm 144 :

"That our garners may be full, affording all manner of store : that our sheep may bring forth thousands and ten thousands in our streets : That our oxen may be strong to labour; that there be no breaking in, nor going out; that there be no complaining in our streets. Happy is that people, that is in such a case: yea, happy is that people, whose God is the Lord" (Psalm 144:13–15).

Even though Britain is now rapidly repudiating its Christian past, the generally high quality of life which we still enjoy is due to the ongoing providential blessing of God upon a nation where His name has been highly honoured in the past, and where a small praying remnant is still holding back the flood of a crushing judgement. The power of the gospel has been so great in previous generations that we are still living on the residual capital of the salt and light which Biblical Christianity inevitably brings to any society. By a miracle of God's grace, there still remains with us the embers of a Bible-based Christian civilisation, but for how much longer? The journalist Peter Hitchens has stated :

"I have visited nearly 60 countries … and I have never experienced anything as good as what we have here (in the U.K.) … I am amazed at how relaxed we are about giving this away. Our advantages depend very much on our shared past, our inherited traditions, habits and memories. Newcomers can learn them, but only if they come in small enough numbers. Mass immigration means we adapt to them, when they should be adapting to us" [45].

Now, this comment about immigration is surely very reasonable, and to smear it as being right wing or racist is a scurrilous way of dismissing a very serious issue. The liberal establishment, the media and **many** politicians must abandon the crude debating tactic of attacking the characters of those who advocate curbs on immigration. They must realise that when, on the grounds of Scripture, we advocate strict borders controls or denounce the teachings of other religions, we are not remotely being hateful or disrespectful to any individuals in our midst, but are merely setting forth plain Biblical principles which are for the common good.

The Bible makes it clear that all Christ-rejecting religions are false and inspired by Satan [46]. If in the cause of multiculturalism we try to incorporate other religions into our national life, then God simply cannot bless us. He will not share His glory with others who are no true gods [47]. Yes, we are glad to allow freedom of religion, and as Christians we love our neighbours whoever they are, always desiring to live in peace and friendship with those of other faiths, but if on a national and institutional level we set aside Christianity in its unique truth over and against all other religions, then this is a deliberate repudiation of the God who governs the nations. We read of a national leader who in fact took such a tragic course in 1 Kings 11. Solomon became a good liberal; he became a 'sophisticated', 'broadminded', 'multi-faith' leader of his nation. We read,

"Solomon went after Ashtoreth the goddess of the Zidonians, and after Milcom the abomination of the Ammonites ... And the Lord was angry with Solomon, because his heart was turned from the Lord God of Israel" (1 Kings 11:5,9).

The Trinitarian God is angry with nations which fail to honour Him as the unique Governor of this earth and as the world's only Saviour of sinful men. Today Britain desperately needs to hear the Christian gospel, because in the post-war period it has consistently repudiated the one true God in so many ways. We are a nation in gross spiritual darkness, and so there must be given an absolute priority to the preaching of the message of Jesus Christ crucified for sinners, forgetting all the trendy social causes of the secular liberal establishment, but calling instead upon sinners to repent. This gospel of repentance unto salvation is the individual's only hope, and this gospel is our beloved nation's only hope.

The contemporary Indian philosopher and author, Vishal Mangalwadi, has written a book entitled, "The book that changed your world". It is all about the influence of the Bible upon western society. What is particularly fascinating about it is that it comes from someone writing from an Asian and eastern perspective.

Mr Mangalwadi points out that in the post-Reformation period in Europe the translation of the Scriptures into national languages, as opposed to the trans-national language of Latin, had a most beneficial effect upon the development of the national identities of Germany, the Netherlands and Britain. As people read God's word in their own tongue, they became more aware of their identity as a corporate grouping in the sight of God.

After all, as has already been stated, the Old Testament is essentially the account of God's dealings with a specific nation, with a people whom He Himself formed into a nation.

When we read the Bible in our own tongue of how God dealt with the nation of Israel throughout the period covered by the Old Testament, apart from its deep prophetic significance as being preparatory for the appearing on earth of the Lord Jesus Christ, its other immediate application for contemporary readers is, How is God going to deal with our nation today? So the Bible actually encourages us to think in national terms.

Mr. Mangalwadi focuses upon the work of the Christian missionaries who came to his native land in the early 19th century. Their desire was that the indigenous people might have God's word in their own language. So they worked upon bringing system, form and structure to the many Indian dialects. The endeavours of these missionaries became a major factor in the eventual development of the languages of India, Pakistan and Bangladesh.

Hindustani is the root language both of Hindi, the national language of India, and of Urdu, the national language of Pakistan. It was the Christian missionary, Henry Martyn, who first translated the Bible into Hindustani, and it was his pioneering work which helped to consolidate Hindustani into a grammatical and written tongue. So the vital point being made here is that Bible-believing Christian missionaries actually promoted the development of nationhood in Asia.

The missionaries William Carey, Joshua Marsham and

William Ward studied numerous speech-only Indian dialects to create from them literary languages, which could then become mediums to transmit the word of God. In 1809 Carey completed the translation of the Bible into Bengali, which has since become the national language of Bangladesh.

Mr. Mangalwadi writes concerning Carey, Marsham and Ward, "They chose to use Bengali rather than English as the medium of instruction (at their college) ... because they wanted Indians to come ... and find the truth that liberates individuals and builds great nations" [48]. So here we observe how, historically, Bible-believing Christians working abroad have actually promoted national identity in the cause of the Gospel.

Mr. Mangalwadi states perceptively, **"Sovereign nation states serve as a barrier to global totalitarianism"** [49]. God knows men better than they know themselves. He has formed them into nations as a means of restraining them from creating God-rejecting regional, and ultimately, world-wide empires.

We mention these facts about missionary activity and Bible translation to show that the Christian faith, far from discouraging distinctive national awareness, actually helps to foster it. We emphasise this, because in the contemporary secularist West the very concepts of individual nationhood and controlled borders are now set aside in favour of globalist approaches to mankind's problems, which are deemed to be morally superior. Nationhood has also become a discredited concept within most churches, which is this writer's particular concern.

The Bible makes it abundantly clear that God deals with nations as nations. For example, in Isaiah chapters 13 to 23 we have separate prophetic announcements concerning the futures of ten different countries : Babylon, Palestina, Moab, Syria, Ethiopia, Egypt, Edom, Arabia, Judah and Tyre. So God judges individual nations in different ways. Therefore, it is not sinful or 'un-Christian' for those living in any specific nation to have a distinctly national perspective. Furthermore, it needs to be emphasised that the very concept of nationhood ceases to have any meaning, if national borders are not controlled rigorously.

So, we have established that the universal and multinational nature of Christ's spiritual kingdom does not mean that God is no longer interested in the nations as separate entities, or indeed that nations should actually cease to exist, as many in the churches have so unwisely concluded. Nor does it mean that nations are in essence morally inferior institutions. It could not be clearer in the Bible that it was God who has brought the nations into being, and who used the vehicle of nationhood to accomplish His purposes of redemption for the world throughout the Old Testament period. Then, with the ending of the Old Testament theocracy of Israel, this was never a signal for the ending of nationhood itself, nor of God's activity of judging the nations as nations. So Britain, for example, is still answerable to God for all that it does, and its national well-being is still in God's hands.

In Amos chapters 1 and 2 the Lord denounces the transgressions of 8 different countries, 6 of which are Gentile lands. In Jeremiah 25 the Lord tells the prophet :

"Take the wine cup of this fury at my hand, and cause all the nations to whom I send thee to drink it" (Jeremiah 25:15).

He then in the subsequent verses lists numerous kingdoms which are the specific object of God's wrath. We thus observe how the Lord determines the destinies of all peoples according to their nationhood. We also read in Daniel 4 concerning God's universal government of the nations :

"The most High ruleth in the kingdom of men, and giveth it to whomsoever he will" (Daniel 4:25).

Again in the book of Daniel we are given a vivid example of God's sovereignty over national destinies. In chapter 5 we read how the Lord miraculously causes a hand to write on the wall of the palace of Belshazzar, emperor of Babylon. The terrifying words are addressed, not only to the wicked king, but to his nation as a corporate entity. The writing declares :

"God hath numbered thy kingdom, and finished it … Thou art weighed in the balances, and art found wanting … Thy kingdom is divided, and given to the Medes and Persians" (Daniel 5:26-28).

So Babylon was to fall because God has decreed it. Has this same God in the New Testament period, this God who wielded supreme power over all lands and their rulers in Old Testament times, now ceased to possess such power? Of course not. Indeed, it is said of the ascended Christ in Revelation 19 :

"Out of his mouth goeth a sharp sword, that with it he

should smite the nations: and he shall rule them with a rod of iron: and he treadeth the winepress of the fierceness and wrath of Almighty God" (Revelation 19:15).

Nor must we imagine that this power of Christ over the nations is confined to the time when He comes in final judgement. This is Christ's power right now over 'the heathen', another Biblical term for the nations (in Hebrew *goyim*). He it is to whom the Father said in Psalm 2 :

"Ask of me, and I shall give thee the heathen for thine inheritance, and the uttermost parts of the earth for thy possession. Thou shalt break them with a rod of iron; thou shalt dash them in pieces like a potter's vessel" (Psalm 2:8–9).

We must accordingly tell the people of modern Britain that they are answerable to the ascended Lord Jesus Christ, who continues to govern the nations at this very moment, and nations which rebel against Him will be rebuked by Him with a rod of iron. Babylon's crime was to lift itself up against the Lord of heaven and to worship false gods. Our own nation right now is repudiating its Christian identity. It profanes the Lord's Day, it allows the destruction of life in the womb, and it has corrupted the most ancient ordinance of marriage in order to promote immoral lifestyles in defiance of God's holy laws. How we need to pray earnestly that a God-sent hand will not come down to write upon the walls of our corridors of power and declare :

"Thou art weighed in the balances, and art found wanting … God hath numbered thy kingdom, and finished it" (Daniel 5:27, 26).

If a nation cannot control its borders, it quite simply ceases to be a nation. Many Christians have become seriously confused about this issue, even to the extent of thinking that it is somehow sinful for Britain to prevent people from entering in the country, if for any reason they wish to be here, and when the word 'asylum' is introduced into the equation, the churches generally tend to just roll over and argue that all asylum seekers must be accepted and welcomed on the grounds of compassion, with no further discussion needed.

Any nation can absorb smallish numbers of migrants, who must be treated with an absolute equality, courtesy and respect. There is no justification in Scripture, however, for the wholesale abandonment of nationhood by means of ever-continuing and large-scale inward migration.

To reject the Divine ordinance of nationhood and clearly defined national boundaries, because it represents the spirit of the age to do so, is to promote an anti-God, tower of Babel, New Age and globalist world order, and Christians should accordingly have nothing to do with such seriously un-Biblical notions.

Chapter Three

THE CHURCHES' SUBMISSION TO THE GLOBALIST AGENDA OF CULTURAL MARXISM

Back in May 2007 there was a large rally in Trafalgar Square in London calling for an amnesty for all illegal immigrants in the U.K.. The rally was supported by prominent church figures.

One of them declared, *"We know that there are up to half a million immigrants who are undocumented, and some way should be found for these people who work in our country ... so that their rights are respected"* [50]. Note how the word 'illegal' was toned down to 'undocumented'.

So here we see the issue being presented, not in terms of the morality before God of premeditated criminal activity, but in terms of the 'rights' of those who have deliberately broken the nation's laws. Purposefully to break the law of the land, however, is sinful in God's sight. As Paul tells us,

"Whosoever resisteth the power (i.e. the nation's lawmakers) resisteth the ordinance of God" (Romans 13:2)?

Yet in 2019 129 MPs "signed a pledge to not report suspected illegal migrants to authorities" [51]. This effectively is to aid and abet criminal behaviour, and shows how Godless Parliament has become.

One of the banners on display at the Trafalgar Square rally read, *"Abolish all racist immigration controls"*, the clear implication being that for the Government to control the nation's borders *at all* is racist. This sadly continues to reflect the mindset of so many churches today, many years later as this book is being written.

As Mayor of London, Boris Johnson called for an amnesty for illegal migrants in 2008. The Catholic Church in England and Wales supported the call [52]. In 2018 Mr Johnson, who was then Prime Minister, again called for an amnesty [53]. Then, when he became Prime Minister in July 2019, he once more stated that he wished to consider this course of action. In 2019 it was estimated that there were more than a million people in the country with no legal right to be here. This figure represented an advance on the estimate made in 2001 of some 430,000 illegal entrants [54].

The fact that such a high profile politician as Boris Johnson made these calls shows the high level of moral respectability being accorded in our society to a deliberate act of defying the laws of the land.

The problem of illegal migration has only got worse since 2019, such that in 2023 some 400 hotels up and down the U.K. are full of migrants who have illegally crossed the English Channel in dinghies. This provision of accommodation is costing the taxpayer around £8 million a day [55].

The Government in 2023 introduced measures in an attempt to deal with the crisis via its Illegal Migration Bill. Protestors outside of Parliament, as the bill was being discussed, held up a banner stating, 'Stop the racist, inhuman Migration Bill - Care for Refugees'. The Catholic Social Action Network, amongst other church groups, denounced the bill as "cruel and unworkable". The Archbishop of Canterbury stated that "Britain must have an asylum system based on justice and compassion" [56].

The assumption behind these declarations is that all illegal migrants are refugees fleeing for their lives, and that their choice of the U.K. for a place of refuge must be honoured as being an obvious destination which is thoroughly legitimate and justified. The validity of this assumption will be addressed, as this chapter progresses.

On the matter of asylum-seeking, the Daily Telegraph stated back in 2010, *"In the past decade suspected criminals and fanatics of every description of have flocked into Britain ... they almost never flock out ... It is so easy to claim asylum here"* [57]. What needs to asked is, Is it a Christian virtue for Britain to make claiming asylum such an easy process?

We are not of course suggesting for one moment that all asylum seekers fall into the category of criminals and fanatics, but some may be, and it is a plain fact that coming into the country without formal permission to do so is a crime. It is common knowledge that Britain is a 'soft touch', encouraging many asylum seekers to deliberately pass across other safe countries on their way to the U.K.. The majority of asylum applications fail, and many of the failed applicants nevertheless stay on in the country illegally. The churches seem very reluctant to condemn such law-breaking. Indeed, they have contributed to the environment which has produced the soft touch ethos.

The following is an extract from the magazine of an evangelical mission working in one of our major cities :

"We have had contact with economic migrants from China ... These friends are often exploited, working long hours (and) living ... in fear of arrest and deportation. We have helped with practical issues such as how to arrange medical treatment from GPs and with basic English skills" [58].

Now no one of course should be exploited, but is it a Christian duty to be in sympathy with those who are living in fear of arrest and deportation? Surely only such fear exists, when there is no legal right to be here in the first place? And if people be here illegally, should Christians be helping them, as they continue in defiance of God-ordained laws?

On May 9th 2010 in Westminster Abbey there was a thanksgiving service to mark the 60th anniversary of the Schuman Declaration, the founding document of the European Union. Seeing that the EU is an institution whose very ethos is the abolition of national borders and the dilution of national independence, this service aptly symbolised the approach of many churches to the whole immigration/nationhood issue.

Churches have accordingly not been slow to use the word 'racist' to describe those who have dared to criticise the high levels of entry into Britain. However, would they be willing to denounce as racist African and Asian nations which desire to maintain their distinctive ethnocultural identities, or, for that matter, U.K. immigrant communities which wish to do so? One suspects not.

Pope Francis, who took up his pontificate in 2013, has made concern for migrants a primary theme of his tenure in his influential office. In 2015 he argued that migration ought to be a free choice [59]. It appears, therefore, that he advocates that, if large numbers of people wish to go and live in another country anywhere in the world, they should be allowed to do so without any barriers being erected to prevent them. So the implication is surely that open borders constitute a virtuous Christian principle which should be embraced across the globe. In response to this, it must be asserted that such a viewpoint has no foundation in God's word, the Bible.

The Pope went on to speak of the need to construct bridges and not walls, expanding channels for a safe and regular migration" [60]. The use of the word 'regular' surely implies that major movements of people's across national boundaries should be seen as the norm.

Speaking to mark the World Day of Migrants and Refugees, Francis further stated that "economic colonialism, the plundering of people's resources and

49

the devastation of our common home" are some of the driving forces behind forced migration [61].

Here, sadly, the Pope appears to be following the classic woke and Marxist agenda, not only of climate change alarmism, but also in respect of the poverty of various lesser developed nations being blamed on the callousness of uncaring western nations. Such a notion, however, is again in opposition to the Biblical teaching that the economic well-being and social stability of any nation is an aspect of the providence of God, who deals with all the peoples of the world according to the same principles, looking to see if they are honouring Him in their national (as well as in their personal and individual) lives. We thus read in Psalm 33:12,

"Blessed is the people whose God is the Lord" (Psalm 33:12).

In 2016 during Donald Trump's campaign to become U.S. President, Pope Francis claimed that the latter's desire to build of a border wall on America's southern border was "not Christian" [62]. In 2019 he again condemned the principle of walls being built to keep out migrants [63], once more an obvious reference to the President and his endeavours to stop the enormous flow of illegal migrants into the USA in southern Texas.

The scale of the problems being faced by that state is eye-watering. In just one day in December 2023 over 14,000 people crossed the border without any official right to do so. Between December 1st and 18th of 2023 there were 167,000 attempts to enter the U.S. illegally from Mexico. Similarly, in the first 17 days of November of the same year 130,000 migrants sought access into the country [64]. It is hard to begin to conceive of the enormous pressures upon local communities and the general infrastructure in southern Texas as a result of such influxes.

Such remarks by the worldwide head of the Roman Catholic Church condemning the attempts by a government to prevent widespread criminal activity taking place on its own borders demonstrate the tragedy across the denominational spectrum of so many churches feebly following the philosophical fashions of the moment, which the word of God tells them that they must never do. The Pope's stance is quite simply that of the political Left, which has no sympathy whatsoever with Biblical Christianity.

Accordingly, there is no discussion at all by the Left on the morality of illegal entry. Rather, the mainstream media, along with the Left-leaning political establishment, focus on the actions of the people smugglers and the physical dangers which illegal migrants face in crossing the Mediterranean or the English Channel. Their emphasis is on facilitating migrant entry, so as to remove the potential dangers to them in their risk-taking journeys; and so the migrants are presented as being the hopeless victims of the people smugglers. The Left, along with worldly church leaders, never speak of simple and direct measures to prevent the migrants coming in the first place, such as the U.K. leaving the European Court of Human Rights, or doing what Australia did when faced with a similar problem, making it known that anyone making payments to people smugglers in order to gain illegal access to the country would immediately thwart any right to settle in Australia [65].

For the mainstream politicians (including those who go under the name 'Conservative') a naval blockade to stop the criminal flow of migrants would be unthinkable, and indeed morally repugnant. As the journalist Robert James, speaking on this issue has stated, "(There is a) huge drive of the globalising Left to render nation states powerless to control their own borders … The Left's approach to the migrant crisis is analogous to their approach to drugs : they want to legalise and normalise it, and hide this aim behind rhetoric about bringing the profiteers (the people traffickers) to book" [66].

In September 2023 Pope Francis visited Marseille, a key area on France's southern coast in respect of migrants heading from the Middle East and North Africa across the Mediterranean and into Italy, and then moving on into France. In many cases France will also be viewed as a mere stepping stone for ultimate entry into the U.K., the most cherished, it appears, of possible destinations. One of the places which the migrants aim for is Ventimiglia in northern Italy close to the border with France and around 200 kilometres from Marseille. Here they hope to enter France illegally across various mountain passes [67]. Francis focused upon immigration during his visit to Marseille, and stated that the primary need was to show humanity and compassion to the migrants, the clear implication of his words being that for countries to protect their borders and prohibit entry is quite simply immoral and unacceptable.

The Guardian newspaper reported on the Pope's visit that his "position on migration stands in contrast to some countries in Europe that are emphasising border fences, repatriations and the possibility of a naval blockade to keep refugees out" [68]. Indeed, the Pope has criticised European nations for not being more accepting of large scale migration, speaking of them as those "who live in their bubble (and) in a culture of prosperity" [69].

So we observe here how a major church leader with worldwide influence is presenting the whole migration debate very much in terms of the indifference of the rich to the plight of the poor and of a failure by Europe and other western nations to show enough compassion. It is this emotive and simplistic response, which perfectly accords with the worldview of cultural Marxism, and so it must be rigorously challenged.

What about, for example, the need for the individual nations where poverty and social unrest prevail endeavouring to sort out the situation in their own lands, so that their people do not wish to leave? In such circumstances there is indeed a good argument for economic aid to be granted by richer nations to help sort these issues out. However, the problems of war, poverty and social instability in the world cannot simply be removed by means of mass and permanent movements of peoples from one continent to another incorporating, as it inevitably does, the ignoring and indeed despising of the integrity of God-ordained national borders.

Yes, of course, there may at times be the need for temporary flight from very dangerous war zones, but that should take the form of escaping to the very nearest safe regions and to the establishment of internationally administered refugee camps. Permanent migration across continents, however, is not the solution, and if a few thousand migrants from a certain country should be allowed to enter into other richer countries on the grounds that they are needy and desperate, then the same logic demands that the whole civilian population of that same country should also be allowed to enter. So how many millions are to be received in order to meet the demands of the Marxist interpretation of what constitutes true compassion? Does compassion now demand the obliteration of all national identities and the happy acceptance of the wilful criminal behaviour of entry into other people's lands without any authority to do so?

Shortly before his visit to Marseille in 2023 Pope Francis stated that migration is "essential for the future of all" [70]. This observation presumably means that mass movements of peoples across continents is necessary for the well-being of the whole earth, but, we repeat, there are no Biblical grounds for such a viewpoint, implying as it does that national borders are not a part of God's purposes, which they most definitely are, as we saw in chapter 2.

So, not only church leaders, but the political establishment generally throughout the western world, seem to have adopted the mindset that there is is something deeply unethical about nations in the West rigorously controlling their borders (though, inconsistently, they do not assert this in respect of non-western nations). Therefore we find that the United Nations (U.N.) itself is promoting large-scale migration as being no less than a source of great benefit for the whole world. The General Secretary of the U.N., Antonio Guterres, has written, "Migration powers economic growth, reduces inequalities and connects diverse societies" [71].

The stance of the U.N. here appears to imply that lower levels of prosperity in various parts of the world exposes a moral issue about which the West must take responsibility and feel guilty. Surely, however, each individual nation and government must take the primary responsibility for the welfare of its own citizens? That is the Biblical principle, namely that God deals with separate nations in their own right, according to the degree to which they honour Him. This is what the Lord said to Old Testament Israel about the beneficial effects of honouring God's commandments in their national life,

"This is your wisdom and your understanding in the sight of the nations, which shall hear all these statutes, and say, Surely this great nation is a wise and understanding people. For what nation is there so great, who hath God so nigh unto them, as the LORD our God is in all things that we call upon him for? And what nation is there so great, that hath statutes and judgments so righteous as all this law, which I set before you this day?" (Deuteronomy 4:6–8).

Yes of course as Christians in the West we desire to help with emergency aid those in immediate dire need and to adopt sensible foreign aid policies, whereby the governments of poorer countries are helped to build up their long-term infrastructures, but that is not the same as arguing that societies where endemic low standards of living prevail can only be helped by large numbers of people forever leaving those societies to go to the West.

It is also worth remembering that western prosperity did not just happen overnight, nor did it just land fortuitously into our laps, and nor was it simply the result of colonial exploitation, as Marxism would tell us. It takes generations of work and struggle for a nation to build up its infrastructures, work practices, social structures and ways of thinking so as to fashion an environment of stability and a rising quality of life. By God's grace in Britain and over a long period of time, each subsequent generation has benefitted in terms of social improvement from the labours of the generation which went before.

From the perspective of the United Kingdom, and using as an analogy the permeating work of salt as a purifier of meat, this nation's transformation into the status of a 'developed' nation, owes an enormous amount to the gradually pervasive effect for good of the Evangelical Awakening in the 18th century. Widespread and powerful gospel preaching saved the country from a violent social revolution such as occurred in France in 1789, and it helped to transform the lives of many ordinary people, who certainly by today's standards would be classified as living in abject poverty.

This revival of true Christianity led in the 19th century to the many social and political reforms which improved the general quality of life in the nation, and which we now just take for granted, but these reforms were inspired to a large degree by the labours of Bible-believing Christians. As the Industrial Revolution became more and more a part of the national scene, this permeating 'salty' influence of the gospel made people realise, for example, that workers in the newly springing up mines and factories needed reasonable conditions in which to work and a limit to the number of hours which they had to put in.

The national transformation was a long, hard process - it did not occur overnight. In the 20th century the inherited social stability of Britain helped it to endure two deeply enervating world wars, the latter of which included a miraculous deliverance from a powerful invader in 1940.

The point in relating all of this is to emphasise that it is God's providence which determines how nations fare. A nation's economic prosperity and quality of life are closely connected to its standing as a nation before the Trinitarian God, as the Bible of course plainly teaches. So the solution for nations where there is much poverty and social instability today is not the mass exodus of people from those nations. It is rather the spiritual transformation of individual societies by means of the Christian gospel.

It is fashionable and politically correct to argue that much immigration inevitably brings economic benefit to any host nation. In response to this assertion, it must be repeated that it is the providence of God which determines the economic well-being of nations. We read, for example, in Deuteronomy 28,

"And it shall come to pass, if thou shalt hearken diligently unto the voice of the Lord thy God, to observe and to do all his commandments which I command thee this day, that the Lord thy God will set thee on high above all nations of the earth ... Blessed shalt thou be in the city, and blessed shalt thou be in the field. Blessed shall be the fruit of thy body, and the fruit of thy ground, and the fruit of thy cattle, the increase of thy kine, and the flocks of thy sheep. Blessed shall be thy basket and thy store" (Deuteronomy 28:1–5).

So we repeat that the Bible nowhere sanctions permanent mass movements of peoples across continents as the God-ordained means of tackling poverty and inequality in every age. The logic of such a position is that any nation which does not enjoy as high a standard of living, as, say, western Europe or the USA, must of necessity denude itself of its most productive citizens as they flee to the West, even though they are the very ones who could be at the forefront of turning around for good the situation in their own countries.

Regarding Mr Guterres's view that mass immigration leads to the "connecting of diverse societies", this seems to be another way of saying that it is morally preferable for all the nations of the world to lose their distinctive identities in pursuit of the diversity which mass immigration brings.

However, this pursuit of diversity tends to be one-way traffic. It is not all nations of the world which are being encouraged to embrace diversity, only the highly developed western societies which have possessed broadly Christianity-based civilisations. For example, as Islamic culture grows increasingly influential in Europe, traditional Islamic countries are not at the same time themselves becoming more diverse, nor do they wish to be, nor is the politically correct liberal establishment in the West arguing that they should be.

Mr Guterres further argues, *"Migrants make huge contributions to both their host countries and countries of origin"* [72]. This latter benefit is achieved, we are told, by substantial remittances of money being sent home by migrants. However, may one respectfully ask here, If migrants to Europe are able to leave behind their families in their countries of origin, even temporarily, can the situation in those countries be so desperate as to justify the demand for compassion which so many argue must motivate the West's opening of their borders to them in the first place?

Mr Guterres goes on to say that governments which erect obstacles to migration harm their own economies and encourage illegal immigration: *"Aspiring migrants, denied legal pathways to travel, inevitably fall back on irregular methods"* [73].

This seems to be blaming the law-maker for the actions of the law-breaker. It does not appear to occur to the United Nations that it might actually be morally wrong deliberately to break the laws of another land by trying to enter into it. Should we all leave our homes unlocked at night with signs outside saying, *'If you think you are needy, please come into the house and take whatever you want. We give you permission, because we dislike the laws which criminalise theft'*. How is such a sign any different in spirit to what appears to be the stance of the U.N. on migration?

In December 2017 the European Commissioner for Migration, Home Affairs and Citizenship, Mr Dimitris Avramopoulos, wrote, "At the end of the day, we all need to be ready to accept migration, mobility and diversity as the new norm" [74]. So it appears that Europe's political leaders are arguing that mass immigration is one of the inevitabilities of modern life, just like supermarkets or traffic jams, and that it is backward-looking to debate or even question it. The

Commissioner also commented that large-scale migration is "an economic and social imperative for our ageing continent" [75].

As a Bible-believing Christian here, one might suggest that if the continent needs more young people, it could start by not aborting its own offspring in the womb, and it could also abandon the feminism which tends to downplay the importance of motherhood and home-making.

Mr Avramopoulos further tells us that the recent discourse on migration — influenced by rising nationalism, populism and xenophobia — has limited our opportunities to put in place smart, forward-looking migration policies [76]. This attempt by the European Union to make the very concept of controlled borders into a moral wickedness inspired by xenophobia (as opposed to common sense) has tended to reflect the position of many U.K. churches also.

As previously stated, the very principles of nationhood and controlled borders are part of God's purposes for mankind. Bible-believing Christians, therefore, have tended to view with thanksgiving the referendum vote back in June 2016 for Britain to leave the European Union. This was surely a wonderful God-given reprieve, and an indication that the Lord is still being gracious to an undeserving nation.

However, since the referendum there have been many voices expressing doubts about the wisdom of the referendum outcome. Many in our nation still do not grasp the fundamental importance of nationhood. Many churches also have imbibed the spirit of the age, and so frequently suggest that any emphasis by politicians upon nationhood must by definition be xenophobic, right wing and intrinsically 'un-Christian'. This all-pervading embrace of anti-Christian cultural Marxism within the churches must be challenged. In Colossians 2:8 the apostle Paul writes,

"Beware lest any man spoil you through philosophy and vain deceit, after the tradition of men, after the rudiments of the world, and not after Christ" (Colossians 2:8).

Here is a direct warning in God's word that Christians should not turn to man-made secular philosophy and dress it up as Christian teaching. Yet this is precisely what the churches have done over the last 60 years, feebly emulating establishment thinking and the political Left in their advocacy of mass migration, and in their adoption of the highly successful liberal tactic of denouncing as racist anyone who disagrees with the pro-immigration agenda.

Those who uphold the Biblical ordinance of nationhood really are up against 'the world' on this issue, using that latter term both in its theological sense of all those outside of the kingdom of God, and also in its more literal sense of the majority of people everywhere. When churches emulate the pc orthodoxy of the moment, Scripture-honouring Christians should always be on their guard, because the word of God further warns,

"*Be not conformed to this world*" *(Romans 12:2),* and *"whosoever therefore will be a friend of the world is the enemy of God" (James 4:4).*

On May 10th 2023 in the House of Lords Justin Welby, the Archbishop of Canterbury, attacked the Government's attempts to deal with the ever-continuing problem of small boats illegally bringing asylum seekers into southern England from the coast of France.

He argued that Britain should only deal with the crisis by means of international agreements, not by acting independently as a sovereign nation trying to protect its own borders. He referred to the migrants coming into the country without any permission to do so as 'refugees' who were escaping conflict and the effects of climate change. He described the Government's proposed legislation to stop the never-ending flow of illegal entrants, and to deport those thus entering, as a failure of Britain to meet its moral responsibilities [77]. His views, supported by other bishops, are typical of the way in which so many churches have capitulated to the spirit of the age, fashioned as it is by many years of the march of the cultural Marxists through our national institutions.

Justin Welby appears to have no regard for the clearly stated Biblical principle that all people are under an obligation to keep the laws of the land (Romans 13:1-4, 1 Peter 2:13-14), and that those laws include respecting a nation's borders. In other words, to deliberately attempt to bypass Britain's immigration laws is sinful in God's sight.

As a Bible-honouring Christian minister, this writer feels obliged to denounce the virtue-signalling and tedious playing of the compassion card by the liberal establishment, including church leaders, concerning the crisis which is the premeditated criminal activity of small boats packed with asylum seekers crossing the English Channel almost every day.

Are illegal migrants who have already found the financial resources, and exercised the planning and diligence to travel enormous distances across various other countries, really those whom it is our absolute moral duty to help? It is an obvious and oft-repeated fact, but France is a safe country from which there is no necessity to flee. The migrants choose to come to Britain, because they know that, once here, the chances of their ever being removed are miniscule.

Concerning the argument that asylum-seeking is all about fleeing persecution, if someone is trying to escape from a rampaging bull in a field, he runs to the next field. He does not carry on running across four or five extra fields. Having reached the fifth field, to claim that he was still fleeing for his life would simply not be truthful.

One cannot help but notice that U.K. politicians, the media and church leaders are happy to condemn the people smugglers involved in the illegal cross-Channel traffic, but few appear willing to acknowledge the fact that the people smugglers only operate because they have willing customers. In terms of the sinfulness of actions before God, there is actually no difference between running a people-smuggling service and choosing to pay those who run the service in order to benefit from it.

Furthermore, it is necessary to ask if the church leaders who speak much about the need for compassion are

63

willing to condemn the criminal act of asylum seekers in destroying their identity papers before they reach the shores of southern England? As the Migration Watch website informs us, "Deliberate destruction of documentation by tens of thousands crossing the Channel in boats without prior permission must be treated as prima facie evidence of asylum abuse" [78].

This abandonment of legally required identification by asylum seekers (along with the disposal of their mobile phones) obviously exacerbates this problem of rightly processing asylum applications, but the Crown Prosecution Service 'seems increasingly unwilling to prosecute (such) offences' [79].

It is necessary to repeat the point that the migrants know that even if their claim is finally rejected, the chances of their being expelled from the country are very low. At one stage during this whole sorry saga, out of 20,605 migrants who had had their asylum claims rejected, only 21 had actually been deported [80].

This problem of ongoing illegal entry into Britain is taking place against a background of enormous and continuing levels of legal immigration. Just where are all the arrivals expected to go in this small and already densely populated island? What about the pressures on our housing stock? We live in age when many people are concerned environmentalists and eco-activists. May we ask, How many more of Britain's green fields must be concreted over to accommodate the hundreds of thousands of new arrivals each year? What about the strains upon the NHS and our infrastructure? What about the ever-growing bill for the British taxpayer? Do not these concerns also come under the scope of Christian compassion?

In his speech in the House of Lords in May 2023 the Archbishop stated, 'In Matthew chapter 25 Jesus calls us to welcome the stranger' [81]. This statement sadly represents an abuse of Scripture in order to conform once more to the fashionable agenda of Britain's new religion of cultural Marxism.

The Lord's words in Matthew 25 were not remotely referring to a situation whereby thousands of illegal migrants were coming into a nation every year. The Lord is actually referring to the need to help one's oppressed fellow Christians, those who are ostracised in society and persecuted, precisely because they are Christians. He is speaking of those whom in verse 40 of the chapter He refers to as 'my brethren'. Each believer has an obligation to help his fellow-believers in need, including those who have been forced to leave their homelands. So the Lord teaches,

"I was an hungred, and ye gave me meat. I was thirsty, and ye gave me drink. I was a stranger, and ye took me in. Naked, and ye clothed me. I was sick, and y e visited me. I was in prison, and ye came unto me ... Inasmuch as ye have done it unto one of the least of these my brethren, ye have done it unto me" (Matthew 25:35,36,40).

So the Lord is not stating that the stranger, or foreign person, who desires to leave his own country in search of a better standard of living has the right to choose whichever country he wishes, and that he also possesses a special exemption to ignore the laws of the land, which is exactly what the unauthorised entrants into Britain coming across the English Channel are seeking to achieve.

Sadly, Mr Welby's comments about the Channel migrant crisis came fast upon his sermon at King Charles' coronation in May 2023, which was a promotion of the longstanding but serious corruption of the Christian message known as 'the social gospel' [82]. This movement has been prominent since the late 19th century and seeks to merge socialism and Christianity as having essentially the same message. The focus of the social gospel is on equality and people's material circumstances in this world, and this focus is always to the exclusion of telling people that they need to be personally saved from their sins through faith in Christ, that they might then receive the gift of everlasting life.

The Archbishop said in his coronation sermon, 'Jesus Christ announced a kingdom in which the poor and oppressed are freed from the chains of injustice. The blind see. The bruised and broken-hearted are healed' [83]. Whilst endeavouring to expound Luke 4:18-19, the Archbishop quite overlooked the spiritual import of the terms poor, oppressed, blind, bruised and broken-hearted. Instead, he made the Lord's words conform to the 'social justice' message of the liberal, secular establishment. This is what J. C. Ryle, the Bible-believing Anglican Bishop of Liverpool from 1880-1900, rightly says of those verses in Luke 4,

'If we hope to be saved, we must know Jesus as the Friend of the poor in spirit, the Physician of the diseased heart, the Deliverer of the soul in bondage. These are the principal offices He came on earth to fulfil. It is in this light we must learn to know Him ... Without such knowledge we shall die in our sins' [84].

What the good Bishop Ryle was asserting, in accordance with true Biblical teaching, is that society will only improve if individuals are first changed in their hearts by means of repentance from sin and trusting in Christ alone for salvation. It is those who are spiritually blind and bruised by their captivity to sin whom the Lord came to set free. It is the Archbishop's task to tell the world these truths, not to promote the social gospel heresy.

If this author were to meet the Archbishop of Canterbury, he would endeavour to be courteous and respectful. This is not an attack upon his person, but upon fashionable and man-pleasing theology, and upon the abuse of Biblical concepts such as 'compassion' - in respect of asylum seekers - to condone the deliberate breaking of our law, and the rewarding of that law-breaking with generous taxpayer-funded benefits, such as very costly hotel accommodation. In order to defend the integrity of the Christian gospel, Mr Welby's woke 'social justice' message must be rejected, for it represents a mere conformity to the spirit of the age, and such conformity is explicitly condemned in God's word.

One of the pioneers of modern New Age thinking was Helena Blavatsky (1831-1891), who co-founded the Theosophical Society. She wrote, "Mankind is essentially of one and the same essence, and that essence is one, whether we call it God or nature". She described the aims of the Theosophical Society as being "to vindicate the importance of the Brahmanical, Buddhist and Zoroastrian philosophies … (and) to form the nucleus of a universal brotherhood of humanity without distinction of race, colour or creed" [85].

These quotations from a convinced occultist and pantheist show that human oneness leading to the dilution of nationhood is not such a 'Christian' concept as many imagine, but tragically, even churches today are being enticed into embracing Mrs Blavatsky's multi-faith notions in the pursuit of one world togetherness.

Human solidarity, however, has always been Satan's ultimate goal for the world, and the error of participating in this goal is the great lesson which must be learnt from the Tower of Babel rebellion against God's authority as recorded in the book of Genesis. The nature of fallen man is such that when he strives for human solidarity as his ultimate objective, such solidarity will inevitably be God-rejecting and multi-faith in character (because to include other gods in one's worship is to reject the one true God who has manifested Himself in the Person of Jesus Christ (see John 5:23).

Some Christians argue that huge levels of immigration afford the Church wonderful evangelistic opportunities, and so should be welcomed on that account. One courteously replies to this common argument that our Lord's injunction is, *"Go ye into all the world and preach the Gospel" (Mark 16:15)*. It is not, *"Get all the world to come to you"*. The Bible nowhere advocates mass immigration in order to facilitate evangelism.

So many churches, then, have exhibited an almost tedious conformity to the dictates of secular liberal humanism in respect of the whole issue of immigration. Indeed, the creation of a harmonious multicultural society has for many become the essence of the faith, as theological liberalism has cast aside the centrality of preaching the gospel, so that sinners might be saved. The Archbishop of Canterbury, Justin Welby, has also stated,

"At the heart of Christian teaching about the human being is that all human beings are of absolutely equal and infinite value, and the language we use must reflect the value of the human being and not treat immigration as just a deep menace that is somehow going to overwhelm a country that has coped with many waves of immigration" [86].

Behind this statement is the notion that the levels of immigration sustained by this nation historically are comparable to the levels experienced in the last 60 years. This line of argument, however, is unsustainable, because the recent levels on influx cannot remotely be compared to, say, the 50,000 Huguenots who came to England after the revocation of the Edict of Nantes in 1685, and many of whom subsequently went to America. Moreover, the Huguenots who remained here seamlessly integrated into Protestant England.

In the past the obvious necessity of integration by the incomer was never questioned, whereas since the 1960s the nation has embraced the completely opposing doctrine of multiculturalism, whereby it is deemed the norm for distinct communities to retain their own culture and identity alongside the host community.

Therefore we respond politely to Mr Welby's comments that they seriously miss the mark, because the equality of all peoples has absolutely nothing to do with a discussion about nation-transforming levels of migration. No one supporting tighter border controls is remotely arguing that immigrants are of less value as human beings.

One asserts most strongly yet again that we love our neighbour whoever he is and wherever he comes from, but that does not mean that Christians should turn a blind eye to the difficulties which large-scale immigration brings, such as wage depression amongst the lower paid, pressures on public services and the cultural transformation of society. Nor is it remotely an extreme right-wing position to want to discuss these very serious issues.

If multicultural societies are a moral imperative before God, then every other country on earth should also be encouraging large-scale immigration. Every country in Africa, Asia, South America and the Middle East should be relaxing border controls in order to eradicate any existing broadly mono-ethnic or mono-cultural identity. The reality, however, is that nations beyond Europe *do* control their borders, and most vigorously at that.

Yes, under the new covenant, God's *spiritual* kingdom is made up of people of every tribe and tongue, but the propriety of retaining national boundaries and national identity is still upheld in the New Testament (Acts 17:26-27, Romans 9:3, Romans 11:1). So it must be repeated that Britain's virtual open doors immigration policy over recent decades does not in any way constitute a conformity to God's will. As the text highlighted below illustrates, yes, the human race is of one blood, but God in His infinite wisdom has also separated men into separate nations with distinct boundaries, and has ordained individual nationhood to be an aspect of His purpose whereby men come to know and trust Him.

> **(God) hath made** of
> one blood **all nations**
> of men for to dwell on all
> the face of the earth,
> **and hath determined**
> the times before appointed,
> and **the bounds of
> their habitation**,
> that they should seek
> the Lord
>
> (Acts 17:26-27)

Chapter Four

DOUBLE STANDARDS

In respect of desiring to control immigration and maintain a distinctive cultural and national identity, Britain often appears to be judged more harshly than many other nations of the world which also see a vital need to restrict the numbers of people entering into their countries. This is a classic case of appalling double standards.

There follow some examples of nations outside of western Europe which, both in the past or at the present time, have endeavoured to protect their distinctive identities by carefully controlling their borders.

Back in 1968 the BBC News reported on the "increasingly draconian" nature of Kenya's immigration policy, and of how foreigners without Kenyan citizenship could only be employed as long as there were no Kenyan nationals to take up any position [87].

This development particularly affected Kenya's Asian population, many of whom felt that they had no choice but to leave the country. The 1968 article cited the example of an Indian who had to close down his haulage firm, because the government would not grant him a licence to operate.

Uganda gained independence from Britain in 1962 and

Kenya in 1963. "Some of the Asians who remained in … (these nations would suffer) from racial and discriminatory treatment under (the) new African regimes … The Africanisation programme, particularly in Kenya, had a huge bearing on Asians, marginalising them in many different ways" [88]. An example of this Africanisation policy was the passing in 1967 in Kenya of the Trade Licensing Act, which excluded non-Kenyan citizens from certain professions and trades [89].

Today, under the Kenya Citizenship and Immigration Act employers must prove that "no Kenyan citizen with the required qualifications is available for the same position" [90]. In other words, Kenyan citizens must have priority for all applications for employment. Does this make Kenya a deeply racist country? Is there worldwide condemnation of Kenya over this matter? Of course not.

However, to what extent are the employment prospects of British citizens taken into account in a similar fashion today in any debate on large-scale immigration into the U.K.?

In India in 2019 the nationalist Hindu government of the Bharartiya Janata Party (BJP) brought into law the Citizenship Amendment Act. This legislation "grants a fast track (into India) to non-Muslim applicants from Afghanistan, Bangladesh and Pakistan" [91]. The BJP particularly desires to protect India's distinctive Hindu identity. So here we see an act of Parliament making religion an issue with regards to the right of entrance into India from other lands. Can one imagine the international outrage were the U.K. to pass such an act?

Since the end of the apartheid era South Africa has been described as 'the rainbow nation', a term which is meant to "encapsulate the unity of multiculturalism and the coming together of many different nations" [92].

However, the Human Rights Watch organisation (HRW) reported in 1998 that "since the 1994 elections South Africa has seem a rising level of xenophobia" [93]. There has been growing resentment over migrants from other African countries because of the resultant effect on the job market and public services. Hostility towards the incomers is even described as being an issue amongst Government officials and the Police. The antagonism extends towards those immigrants in the country both legally and illegally. HRW also stated in 1998 that it "fears that migrants in South Africa will continue to suffer major and systematic human rights abuses" [94].

Moving forward to 2023, a BBC report appearing in November of that year continues to speak of rising xenophobia in South Africa [95]. The Home Affairs Minister, Dr. Aaron Motsoaledi, has expressed a desire to introduce tougher asylum and immigration restrictions, and has stated how it was a mistake for South Africa to have entered into international agreements like the 1951 United Nations Refugee Convention "without seeking exemptions from certain clauses … Dr Motsoaledi is also pushing for people to seek asylum in the first safe country they enter" [96].

Concerning this principle of asylum being limited to the first safe country, if it were implemented in the U.K., it would mean that no one having passed through other

74

safe countries, such as the those involved in the major waves of illegal crossings across the English Channel from northern France (a safe country) could claim asylum in Britain.

It is also significant to note that in the 2021 local elections in Johannesburg and Tshwane that those parties calling for much tighter restrictions on immigration were particularly well supported, and a senior ANC official has described illegal immigrants as exacerbating unemployment and putting undue strain on the taxpayer and on health services [97].

There are some 1 million Zimbabweans living in South Africa. This high level of migration has soured relations between the two countries, with South African politicians expressing their anxiety over the social end economic effects of such a major transfer of peoples [98].

So the response of the South African government to the very real problems which they are facing through large-scale migration, both legal and illegal, is the exactly the kind of response which, when advocated in Britain, is forthrightly denounced as right-wing, xenophobic and lacking in compassion. Have church leaders in the U.K. ever issued strongly worded statements criticising the South African government, one wonders?

Let us now move from South Africa to the Asian continent and the land of Pakistan. In November 2023 HRW reported that "Pakistani authorities have committed widespread abuses against Afghans living in Pakistan to compel their return to Afghanistan" [99].

Almost 1.7 million Afghan migrants and asylum seekers were instructed to leave the country [100]. The expulsion was in the context of serious food shortages in Afghanistan, but also grave economic difficulties in Pakistan [101]. Let us ask again, Have UK church leaders issued strongly worded statements condemning the Pakistani government?

Here is a further example of a non-western country endeavouring to protect its own society and economy, and realising that it cannot just keep on allowing endless numbers of people to enter in from abroad. Yet the mainstream narrative in the U.K., and indeed the wider world, is that strict border controls and deportations of illegal immigrants is the preserve of unpleasant, white-skinned, far-right extremists who have no compassion.

In 2023 a working group attached to the United Nations Human Rights Council claimed that the U.K. is systemically racist, and in particular with regards to people of African descent. It was argued that racism afflicts the criminal justice system, public institutions and the private sector. The group also argued that reparations should be paid by the British government to African nations because of its role in the slave trade in the 17th to the 19th centuries [102].

There are three questions which need to be asked in order to confront the utter weakness and downright insulting nature of such woke claims (which of course so perfectly reflect the anti-white-man spirit of the age in which we live), and they are simply this :

1) Why do the migrants keep on coming to Britain, even risking their lives in flimsy dinghies crossing the English Channel in order to do so? Surely, word would have got around by now what an unpleasant, racist place the U.K. really is?

2) Why is there no mass exodus of immigrants so as to escape all the alleged systemic and structural racism?

3) Which African, Asian or Middle Eastern nation would have endured such society-transforming levels of immigration over a 60 year period such as Britain has undergone with such amazing tolerance and equanimity?

These of course are questions which tend never to be asked, because the nasty indigenous Brits, it appears, just have to accept all the insults hurled at them. After all, they utterly deserve to be insulted because of all their innate white supremacist attitudes (please forgive the author's irony).

Concerning the demand that reparations be paid by Britain over its historic involvement in slave-trading, it is conveniently forgotten that all peoples, races and cultures throughout human history have also been involved in slavery at one time or another [103]. Why is there no demand for reparations from, say, the descendants of the African tribal leaders who sold their African prisoners to the European traders in the first place? A researcher at the University of Ghana, Akosua Perbi, has stated that it was nearly always the case that the Europeans of the 17th and 18th centuries never

77

themselves captured their slaves, but instead purchased already existing slaves being held by African chiefs and wealthy African merchants [104].

Furthermore, the call for reparations to be paid ignores the fact that Britain formally outlawed slavery in Parliament in 1833, and the Royal Navy at much cost subsequently endeavoured to enforce this outlawing around the world. To cite a single example, in 1849 the Navy entered Brazilian waters in order to destroy Brazilian ships employed in the transporting of slaves [105]. So whatever happened to the principle of credit where it is due? Also, are the human rights groups attached to the United Nations demanding reparations from the Islamic nations of the Middle East and North Africa which enslaved more Africans than the western Europeans did? Are they demanding reparations for the million or more Europeans who were enslaved by the marauding Barbary pirates of North Africa in the 16th, 17th and 18th centuries? [106].

Moreover, there is the fact today in the 21st century that there are far more slaves around the world (27 million is one estimate) than were ever taken across the Atlantic by Europeans from the 16th to the early 19th centuries [107]. Yet it appears that it is only the Europeans who must continually be condemned for historic slave-trading. In the prevailing woke spirit of our age, condemning the past colonialism of the white man has become far more important than dealing with the moral wickedness of slavery taking place today before our very eyes in non-European countries.

Moving on now to the issue of illegal immigration, one of the bizarre contentions of the cultural Marxists in Britain, and their friends in the mainstream churches, is that premeditated criminal entry into the country by those who have crossed various safe countries in order to reach the U.K. demands the moral response of helping them as desperate refugees with nowhere else to go.

The reality is rather that large-scale economic migration is being carried out illegally, because it it is well known that Britain is notoriously lax in protecting its borders properly, and that once here, the illegal migrants will have very little chance of ever being deported. This is why many migrants, as they step out of their rubber dinghies on the Kent Coast, wave triumphantly as they do so.

The churches and the Left generally oppose any attempt by the U.K. Government to deport illegal entrants, for example to Rwanda. In January 2024 the Archbishop of Canterbury was continuing to oppose Government legislation introduced in respect of authorising deportations to Rwanda, describing the plans as the U.K. going down "a damaging path" [108]. Church leaders, along with the prevailing orthodoxy in the mainstream establishment, also tend to be against the principle of restricting legal migration, and they always do so on the basis of claiming the moral high ground.

One of the major reasons for this fallacious claim to a superior morality is the enormous influence in our education system and in society generally of Critical Race Theory (CRT), which teaches that America and western European societies are systemically racist, and that all white people have it ingrained into their culture and make-up to behave in a racist way. Growing straight out of anti-Christian Marxist philosophy, CRT asserts that the world is divided up into oppressors and oppressed, and that the white man is by his very nature the oppressor, and all non-white peoples are of necessity their victims.

It is for this reason that any attempt by Britain to have sensible immigration controls and to stop completely illegal immigration is condemned and regarded as stemming from immoral motives tainted by systemic racist attitudes. Yet non-European nations all around the world which see the necessity of rigorous border controls (and so introduce them) escape such condemnation. In Britain's case, however, restricting immigration is simply a matter of a nasty ex-colonial nation seeking to preserve its white supremacy status.

Christian author, Dr. E.S. Williams, in his book, 'Is Antiracism Biblical?' has stated, "The Bible does not speak of the sin of racism, but it does speak of the sin of partiality and the sin of hatred ... Scripture is clear that all people, both black and white (and all others) are sinners by nature and by choice ... and ... prone to hate other people ... The accusation of systemic racism, which only applies to white people, is highly discriminatory and based in hatred towards white people" [109].

Dr Williams goes on to argue that 'racism' and 'racist' are "weaponised words used to inflict reputational damage on those who oppose the wicked ideology of critical race theory" [110].

So the worldview of cultural Marxism that there must be one rule for the white man (the oppressor) and a different rule for the rest of mankind (the oppressed) is not remotely Christian, and it represents an appalling display of double standards. The Bible plainly teaches that all people whatever their skin colour are equally sinners in the sight of God, and must flee to Jesus Christ for salvation. The great tragedy is the involvement of so many churches in the man-pleasing but worldly-wise and wretched manner of thinking which is critical race theory.

Chapter Five

FAILURE TO INTEGRATE

The principle of integration by foreign people into the ways of the host community is clearly taught in the fourth of the Ten Commandments, where God tells the people,

"The seventh day is the sabbath of the LORD thy God : in it thou shalt not do any work, thou, nor thy son, nor thy daughter, thy manservant, nor thy maidservant, nor thy cattle, **nor thy stranger that is within thy gates***" (Exodus 20:10)*

The term 'stranger' refers to "foreign labourers who had settled among the Israelites" [111]. So the obligation to observe a major national religious and cultural practice was placed upon those from other lands who were living in Old Testament Israel. The obligation was imposed by the Lord Himself, who by His very nature only decrees that which is perfectly righteous and just.

The same principle has further divine sanction in, for example, Leviticus chapter 17, where the Israelites are told that all burnt offerings and sacrifices which are to be offered up must be brought to the door of the tabernacle (Israel's temple, before a permanent structure was built by Solomon). The tabernacle was

God's appointed location. Therefore, no sacrificial offering should be made and offered up anywhere else in the whole land. This was in order to prevent sacrifices being made to false gods. This injunction was addressed to *"whatsoever man there be of the house of Israel, or of the strangers which sojourn among you" (Leviticus 17:8)*, in other words, to Israelites, but also to any foreign people living amongst them. Thus we have a clear Biblical statement here that incomers must integrate with the practices of the host nation.

As we now fast-forward to 21st century Britain, with respect to large-scale immigration, a key issue is the real problem on non-integration. Whilst many immigrants have indeed gone out of their way to integrate and must be highly applauded for this, very many others have chosen not to do so. In many cases, the religion of the people of immigrant origin, though they are British citizens, actually prevents them from integrating.

We speak this in love, but it is observable that large numbers of incomers into the U.K., or the descendants of incomers, carry on living amongst their own ethnic groups, in their own communities, speaking their own languages and engaging in their own distinctive cultural practices which are different from those of the country in which they have chosen to reside. Integration with the host community tends to be confined to the level of commercial necessity, but there is not really integration on the profound level of the heart and in terms of deep loyalty and affection.

Indeed, the degree of non-integration is now reaching such proportions that it is leading to the whole character of the nation being dramatically altered. One vivid example is the report in January 2024 of the London Borough of Redbridge opening its council meeting with Islamic prayer and chanting [112]. As the commentator on the video report on this states, for this to happen is actually at odds with the formal and statute-based Christian constitution of this nation. It also represents the host nation having to adjust to the incomers, rather than the other way round. Up and down Britain, in how many other council meetings (which are an aspect of the formal government of the country) is this already, or may this soon become, the normally accepted practice?

Furthermore, and this is the primary contention of this writer, there is no Biblical justification whatsoever for the pursuit of multicultural and multi-faith diversity within society as an end in itself and at the expense of a nation's distinctive Christian identity.

Within immigrant communities there is often a retention of great concern for, and identification with, their respective countries of origin, which in one sense is quite understandable, but again it has to be asked, Is this really integration, which is presumably the most desirable goal? (One again emphasises that to ask such a question implies no lack of love for one's immigrant neighbour).

Is it not the reality that multiculturalism is in fact creating a variety of separate and distinctly identifiable groups within the nation rather than a unified whole? Have not successive governments, scared stiff of controlling the nation's borders properly for fear of being denounced as racist, created a situation whereby immigrant communities tend to take on the role of pressure groups within society advocating their own particular cause and interest, as opposed to blending seamlessly into the nation to create a harmonious single society sharing a common identity?

It is a fact that peoples from overseas who have lived in the U.K. for many years still often call their country of origin 'home'. Immigrants tend to gather in areas where their own ethnic and cultural groups are already living. Why? Because they obviously like living amongst their own kind. They often have no need to integrate much with the society around them, because their own communities are so large that they can interact within that environment, carrying on with their own customs and their own language, even though their chosen place of permanent residence is the U.K..

However, if indigenous white Britons prefer to live amongst their own kind and within their own cultural milieu, the tendency is to denigrate them as xenophobes who are guilty of not embracing the glorious diversity of a modern multicultural society.

The received wisdom of the cultural Marxist establishment is that indigenous Britons have a moral obligation to welcome the cultural diversity which large-scale immigration brings. The presumption always seems to be that that it is the indigenous Britons who must do all the adapting to the different ways of the incomers.

So an Islamic lady walking though the street wearing a niqab or burka must be viewed as an aspect of the rich diversity which is modern Britain. However, such a mode of dress - and one says this most courteously - is actually very alien to the indigenous culture. It can therefore make people feel uncomfortable. Should not the issue of showing sensitivity to other cultures work both ways? Should not those who have voluntarily come to settle in Britain, or even if it were their forbears who chose to do, try as much as they can to conform to the ways of British society?

Those in Britain from other cultures who wear distinctive dress noticeably different from the norm in British society, are they not stating that they are continuing to identify with their own ethnic, religious and cultural origins? Are they not stating that they belong to a certain community, which is not that of the host country, and have no intention of adapting to the host community? Is this approach really compatible with the principle of integration?

In November 2015 Indian Prime Minister, Narenda Modi, visited the U.K., and his trip included going to Wembley Stadium where some 60,000 British Indian people went to greet him. A report on the event states that the crowd referred to Mr Modi as "*their* Prime Minister" [113], and they were proudly waving Indian flags. Indian musicians and dancers performed on the stage.

Now one does not doubt for one moment that those present at this event are good, hard-working British citizens, who contribute much to U.K. society, but one still has to ask, Is not the P.M. of these British citizens, many presumably having been born here, and with full rights to vote in British elections, the leader of the government of the U.K.? Is it appropriate to call the chief politician of a foreign country *"their* own Prime Minister"?

The more general point being made here concerning immigrants into Britain from many different parts of the world is simply that for many it appears that a total integration on the level of heartfelt affection and identification is just not possible, because even second and third generation migrants have no desire to deny who and what they essentially are.

Regarding the very high levels of Islamic migration into Europe, as Christians we love our Muslim neighbours and always seek an absolutely friendly, peaceful and respectful co-existence, but that does not mean that we should be denied the freedom to express legitimate fears about the effects of large-scale Muslim influxes, not least because Islam, as well as being a religion, is also at the same time a radical political ideology and social system.

Furthermore, the Islamic faith lays great stress on the possession of territory. Any land acquired by Muslims in the U.K. becomes part of the umma, or community of Islam worldwide. It can never again revert to non Islamic usage [114]. Islamic doctrine denies the deity of the Lord Jesus Christ and plainly usurps the Son of God's role as the final Prophet to the nations. We state this theological fact because it needs to be made clear, in the context of the viability of multicultural societies, that Christianity and Islam are utterly divergent and incompatible credal systems. Sharia law demands the death penalty, if a Muslim man converts to Christianity, and often demands it for blasphemy as well, which includes any criticism of Mohammed [115].

It is the situation currently in the U.K. that a special charity has had to be set up to protect Muslim converts to Christ, providing safe houses for them, because they are living in fear of violent recriminations against them from radical Muslims [116]. So right now in our land today there are British citizens actually in hiding for no other reason than that they are following the faith which our head of state promised to uphold as an aspect of the crowning ceremony of the British monarch.

In March 2021 in Batley in West Yorkshire an R.E. teacher showed to his pupils a satirical image of Mohammed which had been originally published in the French magazine, Charlie Hebdo. The teacher did so as part of an R.E. lesson. Yes, it was a controversial image, but he was cleared by an independent external investigation of deliberately causing offence. Yet the level of the Islamic protests against him were so intense that he felt unable to return to his job, and indeed felt that the personal danger with which he now felt threatened meant that he and his family has to go and live in hiding outside of the Batley area. He even felt it necessary to change his identity. Two years on from the original incident, he was still living in hiding [117].

This writer engages in frequent open air preaching as a Christian minister. He takes part in conversations with people who utterly reject the teachings of the Christian faith, including both Muslims and atheists. Some from the latter group are quite happy to say the most shocking and insulting things about the Trinitarian God whom Christians worship, prompting this author to say to them on occasions, Would you be willing to speak like that about any other religion? Is it not the case that you are content to say such things to a Christian pastor, because you can be sure that there will be no adverse consequences for your so doing. You are fearless about denouncing Christianity to a Christian preacher's face, because you know that Christians do not aggressively retaliate, but rather endeavour to follow their Lord's teachings in respect of "turning the other cheek" (Luke 6:29).

One of the most precious and cherished doctrines of the whole glorious profundity of the Christian revelation concerns the Person of the Lord Jesus Christ, that He is the eternal Son of God, the Creator of the universe, appearing on earth in human form at a precise point in history to effect the salvation of sinful men. So Jesus Christ is both fully God and fully man, and He must be worshipped as the One who now reigns over this earth in heavenly glory as "Lord of lords and King of kings" (Revelation 17:14).

To deny Christ's divine nature is to the true Christian an act of blasphemy, and deeply offensive, because it is to reject God's own revelation of Himself. Yet Muslims frequently approach this author in the open air and say, Jesus is not God; He is not the Son of God; nowhere in the Bible does he say that he is the Son of God; He is rather just a prophet. For the Christian, however, this rejection of Jesus of Nazareth as God's eternal Son appearing on earth as a man is to reject God Himself, because the Father and the Son are equally divine Persons within the same one Godhead. The Lord Jesus

Christ accordingly declared,

"All men should honour the Son, even as they honour the Father. He that honoureth not the Son honoureth not the Father which hath sent him" (John 5:23)
This writer has often been told by Muslims that the Bible is a lie, is corrupted and simply cannot be trusted. These comments are deeply offensive, and are again blasphemous, because the Bible is God's own word. Nevertheless, the Christian respects the right of his opponents to express such views. This tolerance of opposing opinions is indeed an aspect of the historic influence for good of Christianity upon the general character of life within Britain, and of the Bible's teaching to love one's neighbour. However, is such tolerance reciprocated by those who believe that Mohammed is the final prophet to mankind, and that his creed is unique and absolute truth?

Yes of course, there are very many Muslims who repudiate violence, but there are far fewer who are willing to tolerate public criticism and denial of the cherished teachings of Islam without responding with an indignant desire to cancel and silence those who have made the criticism. This is surely inconsistency, when our Muslim friends in the U.K. enjoy, as has just been stated, the freedom to publicly denounce the key and central doctrines of Biblical Christianity.

The teachings of Islam in their normal accepted form, as laid down in their own sacred texts and traditions, plainly do not facilitate integration into a non-Muslim community, but rather encourage separate development. A simple practical example of this is the existence of around 85 sharia councils in Britain, which are effectively operating a parallel legal system to U.K. law in respect of marriage and family matters [118].

Relevant to the whole issue of non-integration is the following passage in the Quran (which is addressed to Muslim believers) :

Surah 5:51 states, *"O ye who believe, take not the Jews and the Christians for your friends and protectors; they are both friends and protectors to each other. And he amongst you that turns to them (for friendship) is of them. Verily Allah guideth not a people unjust"* [119].

What does this tell us about the viability of a harmonious multicultural, multi-faith society, if Muslim people are instructed by their holy book not to get too close to Jews and Christians?

It is also important to point out that migration into other lands itself plays a central role in Islamic doctrine. Islamic texts teach that Mohammed's migration from Mecca to Medina in 622AD furnishes a model in subsequent ages for migration to non-Islamic countries as a means of furthering Islam. For example, Surah 4:100 of the Koran states :

"He who forsakes his home in the cause of Allah finds in the earth many a refuge, wide and spacious. Should he die as a refugee from home for Allah and his messenger, his reward becomes due" [120].

Surah 8:74 tells us : *"Those who believe and adopt exile (i.e. emigrate) and fight for the faith in the cause of Allah, as well as those who give them asylum and aid, these are *in very truth the believers"* [121].

Two authors and Islam specialists, writing on the Islamic doctrine of migration (or hijrah in Arabic) state : "Mohammed made it clear that migration is a duty that needs to be upheld for ever ... immigration (is) a stepping stone for greater goals ... of transforming the existing community into an Islamic one" [122].

As already intimated, one of the great blessings which Biblical Christianity has brought to this nation is the promotion of religious liberty, which of course includes the freedom to declare Jesus Christ as the only truth, and the inevitable corollary of that, namely that religions which deny that Jesus Christ is the eternal Son of God manifested in the flesh cannot possibly be true.

This author loves his Muslim neighbour, but he must also ask - in love - if Islam becomes the majority faith of the United Kingdom, which is now not unlikely, particularly given the generally large size of Muslim families, what will happen to the freedom to proclaim in public places Jesus Christ as the unique Saviour of mankind and the only way to have fellowship with God the Father? Where in majority Muslim contexts around the world is there at present the freedom for Bible-believing preachers to go onto the high streets? They simply do not exist.

The Open Doors organisation has a ranking of the 50 countries in the world where Christians face the harshest persecution. Of the top ten in this list, in no less than 9 of them the source of the persecution is Islam, which faith is now the fastest growing religion in the U.K. [123].

Both the U.K. and Europe today must realise that the scale of the immigration which it is now encouraging in the cause of multiculturalism and of helping 'refugees' may in fact change the character of Europe permanently and in far more significant ways that its liberal elite political leaders ever originally imagined. A key problem is that those same leaders generally appear to have no understanding of the enormous good which the Christian faith has brought to Britain in fashioning the whole tenor of our civilisation.

On October 7th 2023 a horrific terrorist attack was carried out on Israel by Hamas, the Palestinian Islamist organisation in charge of the government of Gaza. Some 1200 people, including women, children and the elderly, and mainly Israeli citizens, were slaughtered by the terrorists, and some 240 hostages were taken back to Gaza.

The response of the Israeli government to this attack was a declaration of war against Hamas, and an endeavour to remove the organisation from its base and terrorist infrastructure in Gaza. An extended period of conflict ensued. The reaction around the western world to Israel's military strategy has generally taken the form of many protest marches being held in major cities, including London, to condemn Israel's actions as being disproportionate and genocidal in nature. Seas of Palestinian flags were one of the primary features of the marches, which comprised white Britons whose political affiliation is on the hard Left, but also many Muslims opposed to the existence of the state of Israel as a tenet of their faith and as being a gross affront to the rights of the Palestinian people. The British Government's initial support for Israel in response to the October 7th terrorist attack was of course utterly rejected by the marchers.

Concerning at least one of these pro-Palestine marches in London, the Jewish Chronicle reported that some of the leaders of the groups organising the protest actually had links to, or had shown their sympathy for, Hamas and its aims in respect of the nation of Israel. The report stated, "Some of them have been photographed meeting terror chiefs in Gaza, and several have openly expressed support for the violent organisation, in defiance of British law" [124].

One of the banners on display at the pro-Palestine protest in London on November 11th 2023 read, 'Peace is the white man's word - Liberation is ours' [125]. This slogan referred to the need for Palestine to be liberated from its perceived unjust and immoral occupation by Israel. It is important to remember that this banner was being displayed by British citizens and others who have chosen (or their forbears have) to live permanently in the U.K., presumably because of the benefits, advantages and freedoms which accrue to them by virtue of U.K. residency. Yet the banner explicitly separates them from any identification with many of their fellow U.K. citizens, whom they designate as 'the white man'.

So the protestors displaying this particular slogan, and all those supporting the display of it, were actually making ethnicity, as well as their Islamic identity, the grounds of their completely separate status from the indigenous population of the U.K.. This is the complete antithesis of the principle of integration, and makes a mockery of all that multiculturalism is supposed to represent.

These pro-Palestine protests are mentioned simply because they demonstrate that for many immigrants, or their descendants who willingly continue to live in Britain, their primary and heartfelt loyalties actually lie way beyond these shores and in an identity which has nothing to do with this country.

A Canadian journalist covering one of these protests in London estimated that about 75% of the marchers clearly did not have an indigenous British cultural identity, and that they were proudly marching under the banner of a foreign flag : "What I saw is a loyalty to a religion and a political movement that was completely un-British ... what I saw this weekend showed that England itself is being colonised" [126]. This is a fascinating observation from an outsider visiting this country.

Failure to integrate is also seen in the reality that many immigrants strongly retain sentiments of opposition and even hostility to other non-British cultural and religious groups such as were a feature of life in their countries of origin, even when they find themselves living beside those other groups in the U.K.. This has been particularly seen in the English city of Leicester, where the 2021 national census reported that only 40.9% of people in the city identified themselves as white [127].

In September 2022, for example, there were violent

clashes between Hindu and Muslim groups in Leicester leading to the injury of 25 police officers and 47 arrests being made. One newspaper report carried the headline, 'City rocked by sectarian violence' [128]. Again, such a tragic occurrence demonstrates how mass immigration has so often become no more than the transfer to the U.K. of communities from the other side of the world simply in order to carry on living in exactly the same manner as they did before they came, with no adjustment to the new country which they have chosen to reside in.

Therefore the overall issue is surely that large numbers of incomers into Britain have no desire to integrate, and indeed no need to do so, because, quite simply, there are so many of them. They carry on identifying with their own particular ethnic and cultural groups. Even many Christians of immigrant origin adopt the same essential principle of maintaining their original identity with respect to their establishing and attending their own distinctive churches, and participating in worship in their own languages. Would it not be preferable, having made the decision to move to another country, to integrate into existing churches?

In the Old Testament book of Ruth there is a wonderful statement of the principle of integration as being virtuous in God's sight. The Israelites, Elimelech and Naomi, had had to emigrate to the land of Moab because of a famine in Israel. Their elder son, Mahlon, had married Ruth, who was a native of Moab. The intention of Elimelech and Naomi was not that their emigration be permanent, but it did last for 10 years, such was the severity of the famine. Whilst still in Moab

Elimelech died, leaving Naomi, Ruth's mother-in-law, a widow. A Moabitess named Orpah had also married Elimelech and Naomi's other son.

Sadly, with the passing of time, the two sons died as well. When the end of the famine in Israel finally came about, Naomi decided to return to her own country, and Naomi told her two daughters-in-law, who were now also widows, not to come with her, but to remain in their own homeland, and this is what Orpah chose to do. Ruth, however, wanted to go to Israel, although she was a Moabitess. She said to her mother-in-law,

"Intreat me not to leave thee, or to return from following after thee : for whither thou goest, I will go; and where thou lodgest, I will lodge : thy people shall be my people, and thy God my God" (Ruth 1:16).

Let us carefully note Ruth's words. She dearly loved Naomi, her mother-in-law. This family connection was the reason for her wishing to leave her own country, but, along with her desire to be with Naomi, she also spoke passionately of desiring to integrate totally into the life of Israel, to identify with Naomi's people in every way, including embracing the national religion of the land : **"Thy people shall be my people, and thy God my God"**. What a wonderful and important Biblical vindication these words are of the principle of integration.

97

Chapter Six

SUMMARY AND CONCLUSION

We conclude this essay by re-affirming what was stated at the outset, namely that all people are equal in the sight of God, and that the kingdom of God established by the Saviour of sinners, the Lord Jesus Christ, incorporates men out of every nation upon the face of the earth. Furthermore, the Christian endeavours at all times to love his neighbour, whoever he is. So no one should for a moment regard the arguments put forward here as in any way being anti-immigrant people, either individually or corporately.

However, the primary issue is to answer the following two questions,

1) Is to receive never-ending and growing flows of migrants a conformity to God's will?

2) Is it sinful for a nation to control its borders and to severely restrict entry?

If the answer to both these questions is Yes, then the moral obligation to open one's borders must apply to all nations, including those throughout Africa and Asia, and not just to Britain and western European countries. God's moral standards are universal, and do not vary from nation to nation. However, the obligation to have open borders and willingly accept the transforming effects of mass migration is only ever presented by the woke establishment as resting with western nations. This is a bizarre and hypocritical inconsistency.

The Bible unequivocally teaches that there is no justification whatsoever for nations to embrace open doors immigration policies. Furthermore, it is a horrible abuse of Scripture to take its precious teaching on the all-nations make-up of Christ's spiritual kingdom in order to further the globalist and Marxist aims of open borders and the abolition of nationhood. The new covenant has not remotely set aside God's ordinance of the separate nation state, which is a key aspect of His ongoing government of the world.

The nation is in fact the Lord's means of restraining fallen men, whose impulse is to unite in opposition to His authority. After all, Satan is described in the Bible as "the prince of this world" (John 12:31). What always ultimately unites the majority of mankind is the rejection of the exclusive claims of one true Trinitarian God who manifests Himself to the world in the Person of Jesus Christ. Notice the universality of the terms describing opposition to Christ's truth in the following five Bible texts :

*"The god of **this world** hath blinded the minds of them which believe not, lest the light of the glorious gospel of Christ, who is the image of God, should shine unto them" (2 Corinthians 4:4).*

*"Why do **the heathen** (all the Gentile nations) rage, and **the people** (plural noun in the Hebrew) imagine a vain*

*thing? The kings **of the earth** set themselves, and the rulers take counsel together, against the LORD, and against his anointed" (Psalm 2:1–2).*

The Lord told His disciples, *"Ye shall be hated of **all men** for my name's sake" (Matthew 10:22).*
*"We know that we are of God, and **the whole world** lieth in wickedness" (1 John 5:19).*

*"Marvel not, my brethren, if t**he world** hate you" (1 John 3:13).*

When the peoples of the world unite for action, because of the nature of fallen man, the union will inevitably take on an ultimate character of rebellion against the Trinitarian God, and it will also of necessity be a multi-faith union, which must inevitably deny and oppose the exclusive claims of the Lord Jesus Christ (see John 14:6).

Yet churches have openly embraced, because it is fashionable to do so, the globalist agenda of the cultural Marxists, and the notion that a melting pot, 'global village' world order of inter-dependence headed up a single world authority, along with the setting aside of national boundaries and national self-determination, is the ultimate objective and the ultimate virtue.

The stance of mainstream, politically correct opinion, along with the many churches feebly following it, is profoundly inconsistent, because, on the one hand, whilst the separate cultural identity of immigrant communities is strongly asserted and respected, on the other hand, the indigenous white Britons are told that they must suppress their distinctive identity - even to the extent of being ashamed that they are white - and must instead willingly embrace the diversity which the powers that be have imposed upon them as being good for them.

The creation of separate nations with controlled borders has been God's purpose for the world ever since the time of the building of the Tower of Babel, which can be dated to around the year 2242 BC [129]. We have this teaching of God's separating out the nations, not just in the Old Testament (e.g. Deuteronomy 32:8 - *"The most High divided to the nations their inheritance ... He set the bounds of the people"*), but also in the New, where we are told concerning the nations that God *"hath determined the times before appointed, and the bounds of their habitation" (Acts 17:26)*. So clearly defined nations and the extent of their borders are what God has decreed for mankind over millennia, and what He continues to decree today.

In Revelation chapter 7 the apostle John writes,

"I beheld, and, lo, a great multitude, which no man could number, of all nations, and kindreds, and people, and tongues, stood before the throne, and before the Lamb, clothed with white robes, and palms in their hands; And cried with a loud voice, saying, Salvation to our God which sitteth upon the throne, and unto the Lamb" (Revelation 7:9–10).

Here is a picture of the redeemed out of all nations worshipping God around His heavenly throne. It is interesting that the apostle John recognises in his vision, not just an amorphous multitude, but that he is able to identify the presence of many peoples out of every nation. Whilst this teaches us of course that the peoples of the world are all made one though faith in Christ, it is also indicates that national identities do not appear to be obliterated even in the heavenly realm and even despite the unity in Christ.

By God's grace, this author is out on the streets most weeks proclaiming the gospel of Jesus Christ crucified for sinners to peoples of all kinds of races, cultures and religions, including in places which have some of the largest concentration of migrants in the whole country. It makes no difference who the hearers are, for all are equally hopeless sinners and need to hear of the only Saviour, the Lord Jesus Christ.

The gospel is the only hope for this nation, not only in respect of the eternal salvation of men's souls, but also because the righteousness before God which the gospel produces when received by its hearers has an utterly purifying effect upon the well-being of any people, economically, politically and socially.

The nation's primary need, therefore, is to hear the gospel. This, however, does not in any way negate the further urgent need for Britain to control its borders. The restriction of immigration into this small and overcrowded island is an honourable task which is in perfect alignment with the teachings of the Bible (which is this author's only authority). The failure of British governments to do this is a failure of their duty as national leaders who are under the authority of Almighty God, who Himself ordained nationhood.

Seventh Section

Footnotes/References

[1] https://www.conservativewoman.co.uk/soaring-immigration-and-a-government-in-chaotic-denial/

[2] https://www.migrationwatchuk.org/press-release/705

[3] https://www.migrationwatchuk.org/press-article/197/more-than-8000-new-schools-and-162-hospitals-by-2046-the-numbers-that-show-britains-migration-problem-is-spiralling

[4] Ibid.

[5] https://www.migrationwatchuk.org/press-release/705

[6] https://www.theguardian.com/society/2018/jan/11/nhs-winter-crisis-hospital-felt-like-something-out-of-a-war-zone

[7] https://www.ft.com/content/54bd0865-c4f9-43cb-9e76-10da6a1c57e8

[8] Ibid.

[9] https://www.ons.gov.uk/peoplepopulationandcommunity/birthsdeathsandmarriages/livebirths/bulletins/parentscountryofbirthenglandandwales/2022#live-births-to-uk-born-and-non-uk-born-women

[10] https://www.migrationwatchuk.org/key topics/population

[11] https://www.conservativewoman.co.uk/a-stranger-in-my-own-land/

[12] Mayar Tousi TV : https://www.youtube.com/watch?v=69j4S-QWmX0

[13] Joe Baron, https://www.conservativewoman.co.uk/a-stranger-in-my-own-land/

[14] https://www.thesun.co.uk/news/4302003/rotherham-sex-abuse-scandal-child-grooming-exploitation-sarah-champion-mp/amp/

[15] http://www.bbc.co.uk/news/uk-england-south-yorkshire-28939089

[16] https://www.youtube.com/watch?v=00w9HEmiqF8

[17] Murray, Douglas. The Strange Death of Europe : Immigration, Identity, Islam . Bloomsbury Publishing, Kindle Edition.

[18] https://www.migrationwatchuk.org/key-topics/population

[19] Ibid.

[20] http://www.dailymail.co.uk/news/article-2530125/This-worryingly-crowded-isle-England-officially-Europes-densely-packed-country.html

[21] http://www.thetimes.co.uk/edition/news/mystery-solved-in-migration-figures-mismatch-x96ntz8fp

[22] https://assets.publishing.service.gov.uk/government/uploads/system/uploads/attachment_data/file/682491/nino-registrations-adult-overseas-nationals-december-2017-summary.pdf

[23] https://www.gov.uk/government/statistics/national-insurance-numbers-allocated-to-adult-overseas-nationals-to-june-2023/national-insurance-numbers-allocated-to-adult-overseas-nationals-to-june-2023

[24] http://www.dailymail.co.uk/debate/article-2213866/Lord-Carey-When-politicians-realise-racist-actually-DO-immigration.html

[25] http://www.dailymail.co.uk/debate/article-3051489/DAILY-MAIL-COMMENT-Immigration-issue-time-totally-ignored-major-parties.html

[26] https://www.ethnicity-facts-figures.service.gov.uk/uk-population-by-ethnicity/national-and-regional-populations/regional-ethnic-diversity/latest/

[27] https://www.conservativewoman.co.uk/soaring-immigration-and-a-government-in-chaotic-denial/

[28] https://www.migrationwatchuk.org/press-article/197/more-than-8000-new-schools-and-162-hospitals-by-2046-the-numbers-that-show-britains-migration-problem-is-spiralling

[29] https://www.ons.gov.uk/peoplepopulationandcommunity/populationandmigration/internationalmigration/bulletins/longterminternationalmigrationprovisional/yearendingjune2023#:~:text=1.,) and British (84,000).

[30] https://www.migrationwatchuk.org/briefing-paper/424. accessed 01-12-17

[31] https://iasservices.org.uk/how-many-immigrants-are-in-the-uk/#:~:text=As of the year ending,were born outside the EU.

[32] Daily Telegraph, 10/02/2010.

[33] https://www.ukpopulation.org/london-population/#:~:text=59.8% out of the total,Pakistan and 2.7% of Bangladesh.

[34] H. Lacey, God and the Nations, John Ritchie Ltd, p23

[35] H. Lacey, God and the Nations, John Ritchie Ltd, p14

[36] H. Lacey, God and the Nations, John Ritchic Ltd, p23

[37] https://prydain.wordpress.com/keil-and-delitzsch-on-the-old-testament-the-full-set-of-pdfs/

[38] C. F. Keil and F. Delitzsch, Commentary on the Old Testament, Accordance Bible software edition

[39] Ibid.

[40] Ibid.

[41] Charles Ellicott, https://biblehub.com/commentaries/ellicott/genesis/42.htm

[42] Reasons against Separation from C of E, Works of Wesley CD, Providence House Publishers

[43] https://www.gov.uk/asylum-support/eligibility

[44] Matthew Henry's Commentary, Introduction to Isaiah 3, Hendrickson Publishers.

[45] http://www.dailymail.co.uk/debate/article-3223828/PETER-HITCHENS-won-t-save-refugees-destroying-country.html#ixzz4JaetVyIg

[46] John 14:6, Acts 4:12, 1 Corinthians 10:20

[47] Exodus 20:3, Genesis 35:2, 1 Corinthians 8:4-6

[48] V. Mangalwadi, The book that changed your world, p32-33 of chapter 10, Kobo edition

[49] Ibid, p37 of chapter 10, Kobo edition

[50] Daily Telegraph, 08/05/2007

[51] https://www.migrationwatchuk.org/briefing-paper/434/illegal-immigration--key-topic

[52] https://thepoint.gm/africa/gambia/article/uk-churches-back-amnesty-for-illegal-migrants

[53] https://www.telegraph.co.uk/politics/2018/04/24/boris-johnson-challenges-theresa-may-introduce-migrant-amnesty/

[54] https://www.migrationwatchuk.org/press-release/584

[55] https://www.conservativewoman.co.uk/the-lefts-project-to-abolish-borders/

[56] https://www.thetablet.co.uk/news/17344/faith-leaders-unite-in-concern-over-illegal-migration-bill

[57] Daily Telegraph 20/07/2010.

[58] Changing London magazine, Winter 2005

59 https://www.infomigrants.net/en/post/48910/pope-urges-to-build-bridges-not-walls-for-migrants

60 Ibid.

61 Ibid.

62 https://edition.cnn.com/2019/04/01/politics/pope-francis-wall/index.html

63 Ibid.

64 https://www.dailymail.co.uk/news/article-12881409/More-12-600-cross-southern-border-day-highest-HISTORY-migrant-record-smashed-Biden-thousands-waiting-Eagle-Pass.html

65 https://www.telegraph.co.uk/news/2021/11/20/australia-stopped-migrant-boats/

66 https://www.conservativewoman.co.uk/the-lefts-project-to-abolish-borders/

67 https://www.infomigrants.net/en/post/51996/pope-francis-migration-and-the-issue-of-ethics

68 https://www.theguardian.com/world/2023/sep/22/pope-francis-to-preach-tolerance-on-migration-on-marseille-visit

69 https://www.infomigrants.net/en/post/51996/pope-francis-migration-and-the-issue-of-ethics

70 Ibid.

71 https://www.theguardian.com/commentisfree/2018/jan/11/migration-benefit-world-un-global-compact

72 Ibid.

73 Ibid.

74 https://www.politico.eu/article/europe-migration-migrants-are-here-to-stay-refugee-crisis/

75 Ibid.

[76] https://www.politico.eu/article/europe-migration-migrants-are-here-to-stay-refugee-crisis/

[77] https://www.archbishopofcanterbury.org/speaking-writing/speeches/illegal-migration-bill-second-reading-house-lords-speech

[78] https://www.migrationwatchuk.org/news/2021/12/20/deliberate-destruction-of-identity-documents

[79] Ibid.

[80] https://www.migrationwatchuk.org/channel-crossings-tracker

[81] https://www.archbishopofcanterbury.org/speaking-writing/speeches/illegal-migration-bill-second-reading-house-lords-speech

[82] https://www.gotquestions.org/social-gospel.html

[83] https://www.archbishopofcanterbury.org/speaking-writing/speeches/archbishop-canterburys-sermon-coronation-king-charles-iii

[84] https://www.studylight.org/commentaries/eng/ryl/luke-4.html

[85] The Key to Theosophy, H.P. Blavatsky, Theosophical Heritage Classics, p24,25.

[86] http://www.telegraph.co.uk/news/uknews/immigration/11190730/Archbishop-of-Canterbury-condemns-politicians-who-view-immigration-as-a-deep-menace.html

[87] http://news.bbc.co.uk/onthisday/hi/dates/stories/february/4/newsid_2738000/2738629.stm

[88] https://www.desiblitz.com/content/east-african-asians-impact-of-independence-africanisation

[89] https://www.refworld.org/docid/3ae6ab0990.html

[90] https://www.migrationdataportal.org/sites/g/files/tmzbdl251/files/2018-10/Migration%20Governance%20Snapshot-%20Republic%20of%20Kenya.pdf

[91] https://www.migrationpolicy.org/article/india-migration-country-profile

[92] https://en.wikipedia.org/wiki/Rainbow_nation

[93] https://www.hrw.org/legacy/reports98/sareport/Adv5a.htm

[94] Ibid.

[95] https://www.bbc.co.uk/news/world-africa-67405394

[96] Ibid.

[97] Ibid.

[98] https://www.gisreportsonline.com/r/zimbabwe-immigration/

[99] https://www.hrw.org/news/2023/11/28/pakistan-widespread-abuses-force-afghans-leave

[100] https://www.aljazeera.com/news/2023/11/22/whats-wrong-the-silence-of-pakistanis-on-expulsion-of-afghan-refugees

[101] https://foreignpolicy.com/2023/11/01/pakistan-deports-million-afghans-undocumented-migrants/

[102] https://www.independent.co.uk/news/uk/home-news/racism-uk-united-nations-africa-b2270640.html

[103] Thomas Sowell, Black Rednecks and White Liberals, audio version of chapter 3, https://www.youtube.com/watch?v=VWrfjUzYvPo

[104] http://edition.cnn.com/WORLD/9510/ghana_slavery/

[105] Thomas Sowell, Black Rednecks and White Liberals, audio version of chapter 3, https://www.youtube.com/watch?v=VWrfjUzYvPo

[106] Thomas Sowell, Black Rednecks and White Liberals, audio version of chapter 3, https://www.youtube.com/watch?v=VWrfjUzYvPo

[107] Mark J. Perry, https://www.aei.org/carpe-diem/thomas-sowell-on-slavery-and-this-fact-there-are-more-slaves-today-than-were-seized-from-africa-in-four-centuries/

[108] https://www.dailymail.co.uk/news/article-13030513/Archbishop-Canterbury-Justin-Welby-joins-forces-former-judge-Labour-peer-mission-derail-Rwanda-plan.html

[109] Dr. E. S. Williams, Is Antiracism Biblical?, Belmont House Publishing, p93-94

[110] Ibid., p96

[111] C.F. Keil and F. Delitzsch, Commentary on the Old Testament, Accordance Bible software edition

[112] Mayhar Tousi TV, https://www.youtube.com/watch?v=VFzZ3KVr00M

[113] https://www.politico.eu/article/modi-and-cameron-wins-at-wembley/

[114] Faith, Power and Territory, Patrick Sookhdeo, p46, Isaac Publishing

[115] http://www.americanthinker.com/blog/2013/03/ten_key_points_on_islamic_blasphemy_law.html

[116] http://www.safe-haven.org.uk/about/the-plan/

[117] https://www.dailymail.co.uk/news/article-11830621/Teacher-suspended-showing-pupils-cartoon-Prophet-Mohammed-hiding.html

[118] http://www.christianconcern.com/our-concerns/islam/british-police-refer-victims-to-sharia-councils

[119] Quran, Abdullah Yusuf Ali translation, Amana Corporation, p264

[120] Ibid., p218

[121] Ibid., p434

[122] Modern Day Trojan Horse, Sam Solomon & E. Al Maqdisi, p14 and p13, ANM Publishers

[123] https://www.youtube.com/watch?v=h7l9J9-whFg

[124] https://www.thejc.com/news/leaders-of-groups-behind-london-pro-palestinian-march-have-links-to-hamas-ng34ql4i

[125] https://www.gatestoneinstitute.org/20264/hamas-in-london

[126] https://www.rebelnews.com/pro_palestine_demonstrations_london_england_west

[127] https://www.spiked-online.com/2023/09/10/leicester-a-powder-keg-waiting-to-explode/

[128] https://www.dailymail.co.uk/news/article-11238235/Clashes-Hindu-Muslim-mobs-Leicester-expose-tension-one-UKs-diverse-cities.html

[129] https://answersingenesis.org/tower-of-babel/was-the-dispersion-at-babel-a-real-event/

Printed in Great Britain
by Amazon